Judges and Sentencing

CRIME, JUSTICE, AND PUNISHMENT

Judges and Sentencing

Sara Manaugh

Austin Sarat, GENERAL EDITOR

CHELSEA HOUSE PUBLISHERS
Philadelphia

Chelsea House Publishers

Editor in Chief Sally Cheney
Director of Production Kim Shinners
Production Manager Pamela Loos
Art Director Sara Davis
Senior Editor John Ziff

Layout by 21st Century Publishing and
Communications, Inc., New York, N.Y.

First Printing

1 3 5 7 9 8 6 4 2

The Chelsea House World Wide Web address is
http://www.chelseahouse.com

Library of Congress Cataloging-in-Publication Data

Manaugh, Sara
    Judges and sentencing / Sara Manaugh.
        p. cm — (Crime, justice, and punishment)
    Includes bibliographical references and index.
    ISBN 0-7910-4296-0 (alk. paper)
        1. Sentences (Criminal procedure)—United
States—Popular works. 2. Judicial process—
United States—Popular works. I. Title. II. Series.

KF9685.Z9 M36 2001
345.73'0772—dc21
                            2001047258

Contents

CRIME, JUSTICE, AND PUNISHMENT

CAPITAL PUNISHMENT

CHILDREN, VIOLENCE, AND MURDER

CLASSIC CONS AND SWINDLES

CRIMES AGAINST CHILDREN:
CHILD ABUSE AND NEGLECT

CRIMES AGAINST HUMANITY

CYBER CRIMES

DEFENSE LAWYERS

DRUGS, CRIME,
AND CRIMINAL JUSTICE

THE DUTY TO RESCUE

ESPIONAGE AND TREASON

THE FBI

THE FBI'S MOST WANTED

FORENSIC SCIENCE

GANGS AND CRIME

THE GRAND JURY

GREAT PROSECUTIONS

GREAT ROBBERIES

GUNS, CRIME, AND
THE SECOND AMENDMENT

HATE CRIMES

HIGH CRIMES AND MISDEMEANORS:
THE IMPEACHMENT PROCESS

INFAMOUS TRIALS

THE INSANITY DEFENSE

JUDGES AND SENTENCING

THE JURY SYSTEM

JUVENILE CRIME

MAJOR UNSOLVED CRIMES

ORGANIZED CRIME

PAROLE AND PROBATION

PRISONS

PRIVATE INVESTIGATORS
AND BOUNTY HUNTERS

PUNISHMENT AND REHABILITATION

RACE, CRIME, AND PUNISHMENT

REVENGE AND RETRIBUTION

RIGHTS OF THE ACCUSED

SERIAL MURDER

TERRORISM

VICTIMS AND VICTIMS' RIGHTS

WHITE-COLLAR CRIME

Fears and Fascinations:

An Introduction to
Crime, Justice, and Punishment

By Austin Sarat

We live with crime and images of crime all around us. Crime evokes in most of us a deep aversion, a feeling of profound vulnerability, but it also evokes an equally deep fascination. Today, in major American cities the fear of crime is a major fact of life, some would say a disproportionate response to the realities of crime. Yet the fear of crime is real, palpable in the quickened steps and furtive glances of people walking down darkened streets. At the same time, we eagerly follow crime stories on television and in movies. We watch with a "who done it" curiosity, eager to see the illicit deed done, the investigation undertaken, the miscreant brought to justice and given his just deserts. On the streets the presence of crime is a reminder of our own vulnerability and the precariousness of our taken-for-granted rights and freedoms. On television and in the movies the crime story gives us a chance to probe our own darker motives, to ask "Is there a criminal within?" as well as to feel the collective satisfaction of seeing justice done.

Fear and fascination, these two poles of our engagement with crime, are, of course, only part of the story. Crime is, after all, a major social and legal problem, not just an issue of our individual psychology. Politicians today use our fear of, and fascination with, crime for political advantage. How we respond to crime, as well as to the political uses of the crime issue, tells us a lot about who we are as a people as well as what we value and what we tolerate. Is our response compassionate or severe? Do we seek to understand or to punish, to enact an angry vengeance or to rehabilitate and welcome the criminal back into our midst? The CRIME, JUSTICE, AND PUNISHMENT series is designed to explore these themes, to ask why we are fearful and fascinated, to probe the meanings and motivations of crimes and criminals and of our responses to them, and, finally, to ask what we can learn about ourselves and the society in which we live by examining our responses to crime.

Crime is always a challenge to the prevailing normative order and a test of the values and commitments of law-abiding people. It is sometimes a Raskolnikov-like act of defiance, an assertion of the unwillingness of some to live according to the rules of conduct laid out by organized society. In this sense, crime marks the limits of the law and reminds us of law's all-too-regular failures. Yet sometimes there is more desperation than defiance in criminal acts; sometimes they signal a deep pathology or need in the criminal. To confront crime is thus also to come face-to-face with the reality of social difference, of class privilege and extreme deprivation, of race and racism, of children neglected, abandoned, or abused whose response is to enact on others what they have experienced themselves. And occasionally crime, or what is labeled a criminal act, represents a call for justice, an appeal to a higher moral order against the inadequacies of existing law.

Figuring out the meaning of crime and the motivations of criminals and whether crime arises from defiance, desperation, or the appeal for justice is never an easy task. The motivations and meanings of crime are as varied as are the persons who engage in criminal conduct. They are as mysterious as any of the mysteries of the human soul. Yet the desire to know the secrets of crime and the criminal is a strong one, for in that knowledge may lie one step on the road to protection, if not an assurance of one's own personal safety. Nonetheless, as strong as that desire may be, there is no available technology that can allow us to know the whys of crime with much confidence, let alone a scientific certainty. We can, however, capture something about crime by studying the defiance, desperation, and quest for justice that may be associated with it. Books in the CRIME, JUSTICE, AND PUNISHMENT series will take up that challenge. They tell stories of crime and criminals, some famous, most not, some glamorous and exciting, most mundane and commonplace.

This series will, in addition, take a sober look at American criminal justice, at the procedures through which we investigate crimes and identify criminals, at the institutions in which innocence or guilt is determined. In these procedures and institutions we confront the thrill of the chase as well as the challenge of protecting the rights of those who defy our laws. It is through the efficiency and dedication of law enforcement that we might capture the criminal; it is in the rare instances of their corruption or brutality that we feel perhaps our deepest betrayal. Police, prosecutors, defense lawyers, judges, and jurors administer criminal justice and in their daily actions give substance to the guarantees of the Bill of Rights. What is an adversarial system of justice? How does it work? Why do we have it? Books in the CRIME, JUSTICE, AND PUNISHMENT series will examine the thrill of the chase as we seek to capture the criminal. They will also reveal the drama and majesty of the criminal trial as well as the day-to-day reality of a criminal justice system in which trials are the exception and negotiated pleas of guilty are the rule.

When the trial is over or the plea has been entered, when we have separated the innocent from the guilty, the moment of punishment has arrived. The injunction to punish the guilty, to respond to pain inflicted by inflicting pain, is as old as civilization itself. "An eye for an eye and a tooth for a tooth" is a biblical reminder that punishment must measure pain for pain. But our response to the criminal must be better than and different from the crime itself. The biblical admonition, along with the constitutional prohibition of "cruel and unusual punishment," signals that we seek to punish justly and to be just not only in the determination of who can and should be punished, but in how we punish as well. But neither reminder tells us what to do with the wrongdoer. Do we rape the rapist, or burn the home of the arsonist? Surely justice and decency say no. But, if not, then how can and should we punish? In a world in which punishment is neither identical to the crime nor an automatic response to it, choices must be made and we must make them. Books in the CRIME, JUSTICE, AND PUNISHMENT series will examine those choices and the practices, and politics, of punishment. How do we punish and why do we punish as we do? What can we learn about the rationality and appropriateness of today's responses to crime by examining our past and its responses? What works? Is there, and can there be, a just measure of pain?

CRIME, JUSTICE, AND PUNISHMENT brings together books on some of the great themes of human social life. The books in this series capture our fear and fascination with crime and examine our responses to it. They remind us of the deadly seriousness of these subjects. They bring together themes in law, literature, and popular culture to challenge us to think again, to think anew, about subjects that go to the heart of who we are and how we can and will live together.

*   *   *   *   *

When a judge sentences someone for a violation of the law, he or she discharges one of the most awesome powers of the state. In the name of public justice, a citizen loses his or her property, liberty, and, in the most severe cases, perhaps even life. This well-written, lively book examines the sentencing of various kinds of lawbreakers, from white-collar to violent offenders. It combines a broad historical narrative with an up-close look at how judges go about the task of sentencing. Taking up contemporary debates about the nature of punishment and especially the place of judicial discretion in a just system of sentencing, Sara Manaugh has given us a lively and gripping account of one of the most dramatic and consequential parts of the criminal justice system.

INTRODUCTION

On October 10, 1996, a judge in Detroit, Michigan, imposed what she later called the most painful sentence of her career. The case concerned a Japanese citizen, 35-year-old Itsumi Koga, who had drowned her four-month-old son in a pond. Oakland County circuit judge Jessica Cooper spent weeks agonizing over the preparation of the sentence: at least seven months in a psychiatric facility, followed by deportation to Japan, where Koga would be on probation for five years. In handing down the sentence, Judge Cooper told Koga, "There is no sentence I can give you than the one you have given yourself."

No one concerned with the case was satisfied with the sentence. Although they were relieved that the judge didn't hand down the most severe penalty she could have—life in prison without the possibility of parole release—Koga's supporters were worried that being committed to an American institution would be

On October 10, 1996, Judge Jessica Cooper imposed what she later called the most painful sentence of her career; the case concerned a mother who had drowned her four-month-old son in a pond.

13

difficult because of her limited English skills, and thought she should be able simply to return immediately to her family in Japan. On the other hand, the prosecutor, Paul Walton, thought that Koga should have to serve at least two years in prison—not only because the seriousness of her crime merited a harsher sentence, but because "the punishment has to be severe enough to make a person pause before taking a life."

Despite the fact that the sentence appeased no one, most seemed to agree that it was a fair, just, and sensitive outcome to a difficult case. This, in the end, is what every judge strives for—even though having pronounced a fair sentence doesn't make the process any easier. It's perhaps impossible to imagine, without having walked in a judge's shoes, what it's like to have to balance respect for the law with compassion, to weigh all the factors that must play a role in the decision, to try to remain objective and apply the law even as the case stirs all-too-human emotions such as anger, pity, doubt, and fear.

Koga's case was perhaps more wrenching than most: how should one balance the cold-blooded killing of a child with the fact that his maternal killer seemed, because of her evident psychological disorder, not entirely in control of her actions? Although Koga's guilt had already been determined, it still remained for Judge Cooper to decide how the community ought to respond to that guilt. It is certainly possible to imagine another outcome to the case. The judge might have concluded that, while Koga's crime was the product more of her mental illness than of evil intent, murder—particularly of a defenseless infant—calls for severe punishment. She might have imposed a lengthy prison term, arguing that Koga must be prevented from harming anyone else, or that a harsh penalty in this case would serve to deter people in the future from murdering their children, or that stern treatment of murderers would send the clear message that the community would not condone killing. Between the sentence Cooper meted out and the more severe one she could have imposed, who can say for sure which would have been the "right" choice?

In fact, even though this case was by no means ordinary, it illustrates the complex operation that the sentencing process implies. Only in rare instances can the appropriate sentence be determined merely by looking at the crime of which the individual was found guilty. In most cases, the judge must take into account factors that range well beyond the offense itself: the circumstances of the crime; the offender's level of participation (was he or she a leader or a follower?), state of mind at the time of the crime, prior criminal record, age, level of education, family situation, work history, and mental and emotional health; whether the offender abuses drugs or alcohol; whether he or she expresses regret for the offense; and whether he or she is likely to commit more crimes in the future. Not all of these factors will be relevant in all cases—sometimes, in the case of a particularly heinous crime, outside factors will weigh little in the sentencing decision.

The pronouncement of sentence has a crucial, complex, and in many ways misunderstood place in the criminal justice system. It's an indispensable part of every criminal case in which guilt is established, whether by trial or by confession. Yet in some cases, the sentencing may be almost anticlimactic to the onlooker: after a dramatic courtroom trial, when the defendant's guilt hangs in the balance until the jury finally renders its verdict, the sentence seems to serve mainly to give weight to the jury's decision, to lend finality to the criminal proceedings, and most of all to show that punishment inevitably follows crime. To the onlooker, it may appear that the hard work of determining the defendant's guilt has already been accomplished and that the imposition of a sentence is a relatively simple matter of making the punishment fit the crime.

Representations of sentencing in television and the movies reinforce this picture. The sentencing judge is invariably stern and somber as he or she pronounces the guilty party's fate, punctuating the momentous words of the sentence with a single rap of the gavel. This is the central dramatic moment in which the offender comes into direct confrontation with the law's power and majesty, and in which the voice of the law seems to speak directly to the individual. Furthermore, in some versions of this very familiar scene, the judge is often the voice not only of the law, but also of the community. In effect, the community, speaking through the judge, says, "We disapprove of what you've done, and we've figured out how to make you pay for it." The villain is thus defeated, order restored, and justice done.

However, fictional representations don't always accurately capture the reality of sentencing, for three main reasons. First, the individual found guilty of a crime isn't always so easy to see as a villain. Some, like Koga, are obviously more ill than they are evil. Others, clearly, got where they are because of a temporary lapse of good judgment and self-control brought on by greed, anger, peer pressure, jealousy, intoxication, or desperation. Many have become involved in criminal behavior because of a need to support an illegal drug habit. And there are a few who find themselves in trouble because they were in the wrong place at the wrong time, or simply stupid. In these cases, while a judge might not be inclined to show mercy, neither would a judge likely be inclined to "throw the book" at the offender—especially if the crime was the offender's first.

Second, despite their often stern demeanor, judges—like the rest of us—are only human. In a very real way, of course, a judge is the voice of the law; by extension, a judge may also be regarded as the voice of the community, in that by pronouncing sentence a judge is conveying just how seriously a particular legal violation is taken in that community. In order to be

entrusted with the task of sentencing offenders, a judge must appear worthy of assuming the task of speaking for the law. A judge must be especially capable of using the law on the books as well as drawing on principles of fairness and justice in order to come to sensible, equitable decisions.

Nonetheless, each judge, however committed to law and justice, will see the law, the crime, and the criminal through the lens of her or his own unique background, experiences, and beliefs. Inevitably, the individuality of the judge will play a part in the

A jury will render a verdict, but the judge will impose a sentence. It may appear that the jury has done the hard work, but the judge will often agonize over the preparation of a sentence.

Julius and Ethel Rosenberg, convicted in 1951 for giving U.S. atomic bomb secrets to the Soviet Union, became the only civilians in U.S. history executed during peacetime for espionage. Many believe their sentences had more to do with Cold War hysteria than with impartial justice.

decisions the judge makes. That influence may not always be obvious; some judges, however, develop reputations for being either exceptionally severe or unusually merciful. This fact, however we may feel about it, seems to be an unavoidable consequence of the human element of sentencing.

A third reason that the reality and the popular image of sentencing may diverge is the complexity of the factors involved in the sentencing decision. Sentencing is more than just applying a well-defined set of principles to the collection of facts at hand. Punishment is meant to accomplish a purpose, and that purpose is or ought to be part of the sentencing decision. In sentencing Koga, Judge Cooper took into account a range of possible punishment aims, and the sentences that each aim would call for. If she decided that the goal was to make Koga pay for her horrible crime, she might have imposed a far harsher sentence. If she had thought that Koga was dangerous and likely to commit violent crimes in the future, and that the goal of punishment should be to prevent such crimes, Judge Cooper might have come up with a sentence that would have kept Koga from coming into contact with other people for a lengthy period of time. If she believed that the main purpose in punishing Koga was to convince others not to commit the same crime, she might have chosen a severe sentence that would demonstrate to others the legal consequences of infanticide. As it was, Judge Cooper appeared to embrace the idea that the sentence in this case should serve the primary purpose of addressing the psychological disorder behind Koga's crime—in other words, not of punishing, but of reforming or curing.

Any of these possible purposes—and possibly a combination of them—may underlie the punishments that judges impose. Interestingly, though, the emphasis that judges may place on each of these aims has to do not only with the circumstances of each individual case, but also with the political and social values of their community. These values can vary a great deal among communities and can change dramatically over time. As the following chapters will make clear, the central aim of punishment in the United States during the greater part of the 19th and 20th centuries was rehabilitating, or reforming, the criminal. Only relatively recently have judges, in response to changing public attitudes, begun imposing sentences that have less to do with rehabilitation and more with the other purposes of punishment: incapacitating dangerous offenders, punishing them for their crimes, and deterring other potential offenders from similar criminal acts.

An uncomfortable fact underlies these considerations, however. The reality of our overburdened criminal justice system is that many judges must impose dozens of sentences every day, and if they all took the time to consider the purposes of punishment and the unique circumstances of each particular offense and offender, the system would come to a screeching halt. This means that, for many judges, sentencing is more routine and less thoughtful than we may want or expect it to be. We may have good reason to wish—in the interest of justice—that Judge Cooper's experience in imposing punishment on Koga was more typical of the sentencing process.

For all of the above reasons—the complex causes of criminal behavior, the limitations on the judge, and the multiple factors that must be considered in meting out punishment—sentencing is a politically and morally controversial process. It is a particularly pressing issue because not only the fate of the individual, but the very shape and meaning of law as well, can be determined by the sentence a judge imposes. As Judge Irving R. Kaufman once said,

> If the hundreds of American judges who sit on criminal cases were polled as to what was the most trying facet of their jobs, the vast majority would almost certainly answer "Sentencing." In no other judicial function is the judge more alone; no other act of his carries greater potentialities for good or evil than the determination of how society will treat its transgressors.

In other words, the decision of the sentencing judge expresses more than just the judge's (and society's) belief about the seriousness of the crime. It also reveals something about the law itself: is it merciful, just,

Judge Irving R. Kaufman believed the Rosenbergs' crime was "worse than murder" because in giving away the atomic bomb they had, in the judge's view, emboldened the Communists to fight in the bloody Korean War.

compassionate, or cruel? It could be argued that each sentence is like a daub of paint on the law's canvas: it contributes, even if in a small way, to how the law appears to us.

Judge Kaufman was in a good position to speak about the pain, and the large-scale impact, of sentencing. In 1951, he had sentenced Julius and Ethel Rosenberg to death for providing nuclear secrets to the Soviet Union. They were the first peacetime death sentences for espionage ever pronounced in this country. At the time, he explained the sentence in a lengthy statement in which he argued that Mr. and Mrs. Rosenberg's crime was "worse than murder. Plain deliberate contemplated murder is dwarfed in magnitude by comparison" with their crime, since, by giving the Russians the ability to build an atomic bomb, they made possible "the Communist aggression in Korea, with the resultant casualties exceeding 50,000 and who knows but that millions more of innocent people may pay the price. . . . [B]y your betrayal you undoubtedly have altered the course of history to the disadvantage of our country."

Judge Kaufman's sentence ignited a huge controversy around the globe, not least because some people doubted that the Rosenbergs were actually guilty. What is certain is that the sentence, in its unprecedented severity, both was influenced by and contributed to the powerfully anti-Soviet sentiments that prevailed in Cold War–era America.

The vast majority of sentences, of course, don't have such worldwide impact; most are only heard and noticed by a small number of people, and most local-court judges sentence many people every day without having to consider the political implications of their pronouncements. It is safe to say, however, that judges wield a great deal of power when they sentence—not merely over the guilty party, but also over those of us who witness their fate. Many people, both within government and outside it, are aware of this power and have mixed feelings about it. The necessity of imposing sentences on individuals found guilty of crimes goes without saying; whether we've found the best or most just way of coming up with those sentences is a question that has long been debated in this country. In particular, the issue of judicial discretion is one on which we continue to disagree. To what extent does the latitude of judges in determining the appropriate sentence interfere with justice, and to what extent does it make justice possible?

In the chapters that follow, you'll have the opportunity to consider just what the power to pronounce sentence means, how judges came to have it, and how they exercise it. You'll also consider the various arguments for and against the location of power within the judicial branch, and how those arguments have affected the way sentencing works in this country. Underlying these issues are larger questions about the relationship between law and justice. How close does the American practice of sentencing allow our law to approach justice? How might we imagine a sentencing practice that brings the two closer together? As you'll see, the sentencing judge is asked to do much more than make the punishment fit the crime. Rather, the judge is charged with the much more challenging and more politically complicated task of, very literally, doing justice.

A BRIEF HISTORY OF SENTENCING IN AMERICA

"*An eye for and eye, a tooth for a tooth" might have been used to punish this 15th-century criminal. This method might seem fair, but very few crimes lend themselves to this rule.*

"An eye for an eye, a tooth for a tooth" is the famous formulation of the basic relationship between crime and punishment as spelled out in the Old Testament of the Bible. On its face, it's harsh but undeniably fair: if a person commits a wrong against another, that person should be repaid in kind in order to balance the scales. In practice, however, it raises problems (and not just for the unlucky soul who's been assigned the task of taking out the eye or the tooth of the wrongdoer). The fact is, very few crimes lend themselves to the "eye for an eye" rule (also called *lex talionis*, or the law of retaliation). How much sense would it make for a court to punish a burglar by breaking into his home under the cover of night and stealing his belongings? And how would you even go about using *lex talionis* to punish a counterfeiter, a trespasser, or a seller of illegal drugs?

Taking the rule a bit less literally, we understand it to mean that people should be punished in a measure equal to the amount of harm their crimes caused. But figuring out just what punishment fits the crime is no easy task; if it were, we wouldn't need judges to determine and impose sentences.

Every society with even the most rudimentary legal system has judges who are charged with the task of sentencing. Not all of them, however, perform the function in exactly the same way. Even in the United States, our methods and means of sentencing criminals have changed a great deal since colonial times. Our earliest sentencing practices, however, reflect a concern that still consumes us today: how do we allow judges enough discretion to ensure that individualized justice can be done, but not so much discretion that arbitrary sentences result?

The first American colonists came from Great Britain, and so it's not surprising that the legal systems established in the colonies closely resembled, in somewhat simplified form, the system that they had left behind. One interesting feature of both the British and the colonial system was that there was no clear distinction between the legislative and judicial branches of government: the legislature also had the authority to try and sentence criminals. Moreover, most of the criminal prohibitions that the British recognized were imported to the colonies.

Another feature that the British and the colonial system shared in common was that, at least at first, judges meted out sentences based purely upon their own discretion and not upon statutes that defined the penalties for various offenses. This "common law" approach to criminal justice meant that in imposing punishment for the crime of adultery, a colonial judge could require the offender to stand in the town square all day wearing a sign that read "Adulterer"—or the judge could sentence the same person to death by hanging. There was no rule for how judges would decide which sentence to impose, and judges did not need to give their reasons for choosing one over the other. In some cases, people were even punished for offenses that were not formally defined as "crimes." Even if colonists knew that "scandalous speech" was prohibited, they may not have known precisely what kind of speech fell into that category—and they may have found out the hard way. A person could be accused, tried, convicted, and hanged as a witch for any number of alleged "wrongdoings": threatening one's neighbors, bearing a strange mark on one's body, or bewitching animals.

Before long, colonists began to protest the arbitrary administration of criminal justice (as, somewhat later, did their counterparts in England). They resented the fact that uncontrolled judicial discretion meant that they couldn't entirely predict which sorts of behavior were acceptable and which ones could subject them to harsh or even mortal punishment. They wanted the rules set down in books so that they could have fair warning as to what acts were prohibited and how such acts would be punished.

Initially, colonial judges rejected such demands, arguing that they weren't arbitrary in their offices at all; rather, they were God's representatives on earth, interpreting and applying divine law. God, according to their view, did not establish inflexible rules that applied to all thieves or all fornicators; He treated each individual according to his or her own particularities and gave each what he or she deserved.

Whether or not this argument convinced anyone

is unclear, but over time the system of unfettered judicial discretion became unworkable in any event. This was largely because the colonies became more dispersed and expanded to include people who did not belong to the same spiritual communities that had originally founded the settlements. With the growing diversity and dispersal of the population, judges came to recognize that they could not count on everyone in the community to recognize the same divine law or to share the same community values. If they wanted to be able to control the population, the judges realized, it would be necessary to make the rules—and the costs for breaking them—explicit and easily knowable for everyone.

The lawmakers in each colony in turn set out to codify their laws, specifying the punishment for each offense and outlining a range of sentences based upon whether the offender had committed the same crime before. The movement was far from comprehensive: some colonies codified only felonies, completely ignoring the less serious but far more widespread misdemeanor offenses; and some simply stated what acts were prohibited without defining precisely what such acts consisted of. But by the middle of the 17th century, the effort to reduce judicial discretion in the colonies had been largely successful.

Major political and social changes have ensured that the problem of judicial discretion would never be definitively solved, of course. The colonies had, in a sense, a relatively easy job of codifying their criminal laws: the list of prohibited acts was fairly short and manageable, even including the many religious laws—such as those prohibiting blasphemy or working on Sunday—that are no longer on the books in this country. Furthermore, the list of punishments was also relatively limited: most

felonies were punishable by hanging, and lesser offenses would typically be punished by banishment, whipping, fine, or some form of shaming or admonition. Punishment by imprisonment was extremely rare.

Over the course of the next several centuries, as the colonies became the United States and westward expansion began, matters became more

Colonial authorities wanted to control behavior, so they made the rules and the penalties for breaking them easily knowable. This "alewife" is being dunked in the river for watering down the beer served in her tavern.

complicated. Increasing diversity and dispersal of the population meant that greater efforts were required to control the populace, and one inevitable product was the expansion in the criminal law to cover more crimes and more gradations and variations within a single class of crime. Legislatures were faced with the task of producing and defining more and more criminal sanctions, and judges were charged with imposing sentences for acts that were criminalized but imperfectly defined in the penal code.

Another complicating factor was the birth of the penitentiary, which vastly increased the possible range of punishments that judges could impose: not only could a criminal be locked away for any length of time, but the conditions under which the individual was confined—alone in a cell, or in a workhouse, or subjected to corporal punishments—could also be specified. Once prison sentences became favored over other sorts of punishment, problems arose not only for the lawmakers who had to revise the codes but also for judges during the transition. The whole penal landscape had, in effect, changed: if the theft of $5 used to earn a person between 5 and 20 lashes with a whip, what was the equivalent in days behind bars? And if a judge could choose between sentencing a thief to a prison term or a whipping, on what basis would the judge decide between the two?

Largely as a product of these developments, the penal codes have never been comprehensive in their approach to sentencing. But even if comprehensiveness was humanly possible, and even though we may feel legitimately uncomfortable with the degree of discretion that judges still exercise today, the tradition of judicial discretion embedded in this nation's history probably plays a large role in the extent of the judge's sentencing power that endures today. At any rate, sentencing practices today have become by and large uniform and routine. It bears keeping in mind, however, that this was not always so—and that our tangled web of legal history has a powerful if often unnoticed impact on what judges do when they endeavor to make the punishment fit the crime.

The Sentencing Process in the Modern-Day Court

In many a courtroom drama played out on the big or small screen, the judge's pronouncement of the convict's sentence is a momentous scene. Following closely on the climactic moment in which the jury announces its guilty verdict, it lends weight and finality to the narrative of the trial—in effect, it closes the book on the case that began with the commission of the crime.

In the ordinary course of things, the sentencing of a criminal plays a far less dramatic and visible role in the criminal justice system than movies and television programs make it appear. The main reason for this is that the vast majority of criminal cases never even go to trial. In many cases, a person accused of a crime pleads guilty to the offense with which the person has been charged. Another common practice is for the accused to plead guilty to a lesser offense—a crime that's less serious than the one with which the person has been charged—in exchange for a lighter sentence

The judge's sentence, in effect, will close the book on the courtroom drama —the trial—which began with the commission of a crime.

33

than the one he or she would have received if tried and found guilty of the original offense. Finally, an individual may plead no contest—also known as nolo contendere—to a charge, which means that the individual chooses not to dispute the charge but does not admit guilt. In each of these cases, the prosecutor will usually recommend a sentence to the judge—often, that recommendation will have been negotiated by the prosecutor and the accused as part of the plea agreement. The judge will usually accept the prosecutor's recommendation and mete out the proposed sentence.

Why and how do criminal defendants and prosecutors come to such agreements? Often a trial is in neither party's best interest. For one thing, criminal trials, even for relatively minor offenses, are in many cases lengthy and expensive, and so prosecutors may want to avoid using the taxpayers' money in this way whenever appropriate. Furthermore, judges' dockets in most jurisdictions (that is, areas within which a particular court or judicial system exercises power) are already vastly overburdened; if every case went to trial, it would take years and years to decrease this backlog. Since the U.S. Constitution guarantees every citizen the right to a speedy trial, the government has an interest in ensuring that the cases that do go to trial don't end up languishing in the system for long periods. Plea agreements, then, operate like a pressure valve that allows the criminal justice system to function relatively efficiently and justly. In addition, a prosecutor might offer a deal in exchange for information or cooperation that may lead to the arrest and conviction of more dangerous or powerful criminals.

Finally, another reason that a prosecutor may want to avoid a trial is that the state's case against the defendant isn't airtight: the evidence, while pointing to the accused's guilt, may fall short of the reasonable doubt standard that would allow a judge or jury to convict. On the principle that a bird in the hand is worth two in the bush, a prosecutor may decide that it's better to offer a reduced sentence or a reduced charge in exchange for a plea, and ensure that the accused does some jail time, than to take the chance that a judge or jury would not find the defendant guilty of the original charge.

Yet it would seem strange that a person accused of a crime would accept a plea agreement in exchange for a sentencing recommendation, rather than taking the chance that the jury will acquit. Along with the plea comes a certain (if mild) sentence and a criminal record that may seriously limit a person's housing and employment options throughout life. But there are all kinds of reasons that such a deal might seem attractive to a person in this situation; the most obvious reason is that the person is actually guilty of the crime with which he or she has been charged. In this case, the person might believe that he or she wouldn't be able to prevail in a jury trial and that pleading guilty to a lesser offense or in exchange for a mild sentence recommendation is preferable to enduring a lengthy, embarrassing, painful trial and a long prison term. Even if the accused is not guilty, however, the person might believe that the evidence is strong enough to make conviction likely anyway. In either of these cases, the accused is thinking along the same lines as the prosecutor: taking the sure thing is a better bet than rolling the dice and perhaps losing big.

It's useful to understand the many routes by which a convicted criminal may come to stand before the sentencing judge, because the route taken plays a large role in the process by which a judge determines and pronounces the sentence. We may tend to think of the sentencing judge as focused primarily or entirely on facts about the offender and the offense, using only an understanding of the law and of principles of justice and fairness to decide what sentence those facts call for. However, the modern-day sentencing phase is far from the independent, self-contained process that we might view as ideal. Instead, the sentencing judge is only one of many players who have traditionally worked to determine how individual offenders pay for their crimes.

Even before an individual commits a crime or even ponders doing so, the lawmakers of the federal, state, and local governments have already made crucial decisions as to how that future criminal ought to be punished. In fact, it's the legislators who determine whether a particular action is a crime at all. We've seen dramatic shifts during the past centuries in what activities are considered criminal (as opposed to merely irresponsible, immoral, unpleasant, dangerous, or disreputable): not only have some crimes with a moral flavor, such as adultery or using contraception, disappeared from the penal codes of most if not all states, but the sheer number of activities considered criminal has also grown dramatically. The founders of the United States would have been bewildered at the criminal prohibitions against forming monopolies, driving recklessly, selling heroin, and mislabeling food products that were passed in the wake of tumultuous social and economic changes during the 19th and 20th centuries. They would certainly not know what to make of laws against credit card fraud, computer hacking, smoking in public buildings, and joking about bombs during a commercial airline flight—all of which are recent products of our own changing times and responses to new threats to public health, order, and security.

Just as legislators have to enact new criminal laws to keep up with social change, so must they consider and reconsider what sort of penalties should be associated with various crimes. Penal statutes seldom define merely what activities are illegal; they also define what the cost of committing that crime should be. Of course, legislative bodies don't generally assign precise penalties to each crime—if they did, the sentencing process would be very simple. More often, they define a range of possible punishments for a particular category of crime.

Legislatures have used both indirect and direct measures to define this range. They act indirectly by charging or allowing an independent, nonlegislative body to come up with a scheme to determine how judges may approach the sentencing of criminals, which the legislature then adopts and makes the law of the land. Many if not most jurisdictions base their penal statutes at least in part on the Model Penal Code, developed in the mid-20th century by a group of scholars and experts within the American Law Institute. The model code, and the state and local codes that follow it, provide judges with broad guidelines for appropriate sentences based mainly on the severity of the crime and the prior record of the defendant. The code also specifies some other factors that judges may take into account in determining the severity of the sentence. These include the offender's motivation, whether he or she was provoked, whether the offender had otherwise lived a law-abiding life, and whether he or she seems a likely candidate for drug, alcohol, or psychiatric treatment. The judge is not required to take these factors into account, but may use them to justify an unusually lenient or harsh sentence, or an alternative sentence such as mandatory treatment.

Increasingly, legislatures have begun to act more directly in defining sentencing ranges. One way they've done so is by adopting minimum terms for certain crimes that are firmer than the more flexible ones provided by the Model Penal Code. "Mandatory minimum" sentences are usually assigned to crimes that the legislature thinks are particularly grave, but that it believes have not been treated seriously enough by sentencing judges. Drug- and weapon-related offenses are among the crimes that mandatory minimum sentencing laws have addressed, and the minimum sentences provided by these laws tend to be a good deal more severe than those allowed by the Model Penal Code. If the judge is charged with sentencing someone guilty of a crime for which a mandatory minimum sentence is on the books, the judge is restricted—sometimes significantly—in the range of his or her decisions.

For example, if a person is convicted in federal court of carrying a concealed weapon while engaging in a drug transaction, that weapons charge will automatically subject the person to an extra five years in prison in addition to whatever sentence he or she receives for the drug charge. The judge's beliefs about the person's dangerousness, likelihood of committing future crimes, or any other related factor do not allow the judge to alter that five-year figure in computing the sentence. This situation provokes strong feelings, both positive and negative.

While such sentencing strictures can vastly reduce judicial discretion, in the overwhelming majority of cases judges still have a great deal of latitude in how they impose sentence. This is true because mandatory minimum sentences and other forms of strict sentencing guidelines apply only to felonies—relatively serious offenses usually punishable by imprisonment. The bulk of criminal cases are misdemeanors—minor crimes that may be punished by confinement or by fine or other penalty. At this level, judges still may—and do— exercise considerable discretion within the liberal bounds set by the legislature.

Another key figure in the sentencing process is the prosecutor, who represents the government in the case against the accused. The prosecutor exercises a great deal of power whether or not the case goes to trial, although some might argue that the cases that don't get tried are the ones in which the prosecutor wields

Mandatory sentencing laws restrict the judge's range of possible decisions. The confiscated guns in this photo will guarantee their owner a mandatory sentence of 15 years to life in prison.

the most control. That's because, as noted above, the prosecutor is instrumental in negotiating the plea agreement, which often includes not only a determination of what charges to which the defendant will finally plead guilty but also a sentencing recommendation. That is, a defendant might have agreed to plead guilty to a particular offense on the condition that the prosecutor ask the judge to impose a sentence close to the minimum that the law provides for that offense.

A prosecutor represents the government in the case against the accused. This prosecutor points toward a defendant accused of aggravated murder, assault, and kidnapping.

Alternatively, the prosecutor might have accepted an offer by the defendant's attorney to plead guilty to a lesser offense, as long as the defendant serves the maximum term. In either situation, the judge will not be bound by the recommendation—nor even by the agreement struck by defendant and prosecutor. It's within the judge's authority to reject the agreement if either the terms or the way in which they were arrived at seems at odds with justice or fairness. But professional courtesy and an interest in keeping the wheels of the system rolling smoothly lead judges to question prosecutors' bargains only on relatively rare occasions.

When a case does go to trial, the prosecutor doesn't have the same control over the offense of which the defendant is found guilty. After the trial, however, the prosecutor still has the same opportunity to recommend a sentence anywhere in the legally defined range for that offense. The judge may not rely as heavily on such a recommendation as he or she would have if the defendant had pled out, since during a trial the judge has listened to the evidence, observed the defendant, and maybe even heard the defendant testify. Because of this, the judge has been able to draw her or his own conclusion about the seriousness of the offense, the state of mind of the offender, the likelihood that the offender will commit future crimes, and the probability that the offender will benefit from treatment, alternative sentencing, or a second chance. When a guilty plea has been negotiated, the sentencing phase may mark the first time that the judge has laid eyes upon the offender.

It may seem surprising that the probation officer has anything to do with the sentencing phase of the trial, but the probation officer in fact may have a crucial role in determining what sentence the judge imposes. This is because in most felony cases, once guilt is established, the probation officer is charged with investigating the circumstances of the offense and more especially the circumstances of the offender's life and background, and then presenting those findings to the judge in a thorough report. The judge often relies heavily on the presentence investigation report in passing sentence, although—as with the prosecutor's sentencing recommendation—it may be of less value when the judge has been able to gather an impression of the defendant in person at trial.

Particularly in the case of a serious violent crime, the victim might be asked, or the victim may ask, to weigh in on the subject of the sentence. A victim may be the individual who directly suffered at the hands of the defendant, or may be a family member of a deceased victim of a violent crime. It may as often happen that the victim asks for lenient treatment for the offender as that the victim proposes a severe sentence. The victim's input may take the form of a letter, a completed questionnaire (called a victim impact statement), or testimony before the judge at a presentence hearing.

It may seem obvious that we should consider the victim's perspective in the sentencing process. After all, the individual who suffered most at the hands of the convicted offender is arguably most qualified to convey the effects of the offense. Some contend that victims' statements provide invaluable insight into the ramifications of the crime and give the judge a realistic idea as to the criminal's guilt. Moreover, they argue, victims' statements allow victims to confront their assailants, and may introduce an added level of justice to the proceedings.

But others object to the participation of victims in the sentencing process. They call attention to a key principle governing the criminal law: the damage caused by crime is primarily its assault on community norms and public order, and only secondarily its harm to particular victims. Allowing victims to participate in the sentencing process distracts the judge from this central tenet and may allow elements of emotion and vengeance to undermine what should be a rational, principled process. Justice dictates that the severity of the offense, rather than how sympathetic a victim appears in the courtroom, should govern how we punish.

While this issue continues to spark controversy, it's worth noting that victims have only in the last two decades begun to make their voices heard in the sentencing of criminals. It remains to be seen whether this is a valuable tool for the sentencing judge and if so, what place a victim's testimony should play in the sentencing process.

Even though they may not have testified at trial, individuals convicted of a crime are always invited, and often required, to speak on their own behalf at the

presentence hearing. In what is called an allocution, the defendant may say anything he or she likes, and defendants usually take the opportunity to apologize, explain their actions, or ask for mercy. The judge is not required to weigh the defendant's words, but may find that a sincere expression of remorse justifies some leniency. More likely, the judge has formed an opinion of the defendant based on other sources, and the allocution will not weigh very heavily in the sentencing decision.

Probation officers investigate the offender's life and background and report their findings to the judge. The judge will rely on the report while creating a sentence for the offender.

A defendant may speak on his or her behalf in what is called an allocution. Here, actor Robert Downey Jr. addresses the court during his sentencing for a 1999 probation violation.

A more formal request for leniency is often produced and submitted by the defendant's attorney in a memorandum that typically revisits issues raised in the presentence investigation report and suggests reasons that they should be considered carefully. Sometimes this memorandum merely confirms the sentencing agreement that was part of the plea agreement struck with the prosecutor.

From the foregoing, it should be clear that the image of sentencing as a direct confrontation between the judge and the defendant is artificial. Rather, this confrontation happens within a complicated process in which judge and offender come together only briefly or indirectly, and often only after the judge's decision is already made. The huge volume of documents, testimony, and legal rules that the judge must sort through in order to come to a sentence that makes sense and does justice becomes, in a way, a puzzle that the judge assembles into a coherent picture of the offense and the offender. You might say that this picture is what guides the judge in deciding the sentence to impose.

We will now describe the process by which the judge "does justice" in the sentencing process: the theories, considerations, and calculations that fair and just sentencing decisions involve. We'll also see how that process of judgment, like the judicial process itself, isn't an isolated event: it's shaped by politics, social concerns, and changes in the ways that we understand crime and punishment.

How Do Judges
Sentence?

ost local and U.S. district court judges pronounce a vast number of sentences during the course of their careers on the bench. After years in a courtroom, facing similar sorts of crimes and offenders every day, judges become so familiar with the process that it may become virtually routine. Yet all judges from time to time confront cases that do not lend themselves to simple calculations or by-the-book responses. Particularly when the crime is serious, and the punishment is potentially severe, a judge will—or should—feel the burden of his or her responsibility, and approach the task with appropriate care.

What is the process by which a judge confronts this difficult task? We've already looked at the procedure leading up to the pronouncement of sentence, and at the tools and bits of evidence that judges have at their disposal. This chapter explores the delicate balancing act that producing a just and fair sentence involves. It's a performance that involves not just legal considerations, but philosophical, moral, and practical ones as well. And it's a process that, however painstakingly undertaken, is never really perfect: some values and considerations must outweigh others, and occasionally a decision will be based not just on the objective facts at hand but also on the judge's intuition and instinct about the defendant. No matter how subjective the judge's decision-making process, however, a judge is always held accountable for the sentence imposed: in most jurisdictions, the law requires that when a judge pronounces sentence on a serious crime, the judge explain the reasoning behind the sentence chosen.

Probably no two judges, left to their own devices, would use the identical process to determine the appropriate sentence for a given defendant. Most likely, though, a judge will begin by considering the offense and the circumstances under which it was committed. The facts surrounding the case will help to determine the kind of sentence that the offense calls for.

For example, suppose that you are the judge responsible for sentencing a woman who pled guilty to striking and injuring a pedestrian in a crosswalk and then fleeing the scene of the accident in her vehicle. Examining the presentencing investigation report, you note that the defendant had not been under the influence of drugs or alcohol when the accident occurred, but later admitted to having been very tired because she had just worked a double shift at the pharmacy where she is employed. She was found responsible for another car accident five years earlier, but has never had her driver's license revoked or suspended. Skid marks at the scene show that she had hit the brakes prior to hitting the pedestrian; had she not attempted to stop, the victim would likely have been far more seriously injured. Although the defendant fled the scene, and did not call 911 to report the accident, she turned herself in to the police two hours later.

The penal code in your state defines a broad sentencing range for hit-and-run offenses that result in minor injury (but not serious injury or death)—from one month to five years in jail or prison, and from $100 to $5,000 in restitution to the victim. You have to use the facts at hand to decide whether the defendant should receive a sentence that's on the milder or the severer end of the range—or somewhere in the middle. You then sort these facts according to their relevance to your decision. Starting from the assumption that the basic charge for a hit-and-run offense should merit a sentence of average severity—say, two and a half years in prison and $2,500 in restitution—you determine which aspects of the case should go toward lessening the sentence, and which should go toward increasing it. Facts that belong in the first category are called mitigating (or extenuating) circumstances, and facts that belong in the second are called aggravating circumstances.

Among the mitigating circumstances at play in this case are the defendant's efforts to prevent the accident (as shown by her attempt to brake) and her decision, however belated, to turn herself in to the authorities and confess her crime. These factors may incline you toward softening the sentence. But the aggravating circumstances might bear more weight in your decision. The fact that the defendant chose to drive when she was tired and probably not alert enough to drive safely, and the fact that she never called emergency services to report the incident, count against her. The defendant's lack of a prior record, and the fact that she hadn't used drugs or alcohol before getting behind the wheel, don't matter either way for your purposes —they just mark the absence of certain common aggravating circumstances.

It's important to note that the factors that count as

In theory, judges weigh the circumstances of a crime and impose a sentence that will be best for the offender. Lisandra Torres, a former heroin addict, participates in a Youthful Offender program; without the program she might have been using drugs instead of getting her education.

aggravating or mitigating aren't unlimited. The law may list the elements of the offense that should be taken into account when imposing sentence as well as the elements that shouldn't be considered. There's often a "gray area" of factors that may be weighed even if the law hasn't explicitly stated them; on the other hand, a judge may introduce circumstances that later, on appeal, are ruled to be irrelevant to the sentencing decision.

Not so many years ago, judges in this country openly considered aggravating and mitigating circumstances that we would shudder at today. Murderers would receive lighter sentences if the victim was the defendant's unfaithful wife—that is, if the jury could even be persuaded to convict such a defendant. (Angry wives of unfaithful husbands would seldom receive the same judicial courtesy.) And in some parts of the country, a white man who assaulted an African American would automatically be granted a milder sentence than would an African-American man who assaulted a white person. What's considered a relevant factor in determining the seriousness of an offense is just one of the many aspects of the law that continue to change over time.

After weighing the aggravating and mitigating circumstances of the case, you'll have a clearer idea of where the defendant's sentence ought to fall in the range defined in the penal code. But this is only the most basic step in determining the best sentence for any given defendant; you'll also have to consider the case in light of a range of ethical and philosophical questions about punishment, responsibility, and justice.

In a treatise called the *Nicomachean Ethics*, the Greek philosopher Aristotle put forth the idea that the essence of justice is "to treat like things alike, and different things differently." A couple of millennia later, that same idea governs the practice of law and comprises a key element of justice. But as simple as this principle seems, it raises a dilemma for judges that isn't easily resolved.

Aristotle's imperative has two parts: "treating like cases alike" means ensuring that similar crimes committed by similarly situated individuals draw similar sentences—that is, that sentences maintain a degree of uniformity. On the other hand, "treating different cases differently" means paying attention to the aspects of a case that make it unique, and taking measures to make sure that those unique aspects are reflected in the sentence the individual receives. To some extent, penal codes allow judges to follow Aristotle's rule fairly easily. If a defendant is found guilty of rape, the law will prescribe a sentencing range to which all convicted rapists are similarly subject. Further, the penal law generally distinguishes between the rape of an adult and rape of a child, and cases that fall into these two categories will accordingly be treated differently.

But when two defendants are convicted of the same crime, what makes the two cases different enough from one another to warrant different treatment? The list of aggravating and mitigating circumstances with which sentencing judges work is one source of answers to this question. But there are countless other circumstances that may play an important role in determining a just sentence. Think again of your hit-and-run defendant, and now imagine that you were charged with sentencing two more individuals convicted of the same crime. One had committed the offense while leaving the parking lot of a convenience store he had just held up. The other had just left the hospital, where she had been visiting her dying daughter in the cancer ward. Of all three defendants, you may be inclined to punish the fleeing robber most severely for his hit-and-run offense; that offense, connected as it is to another serious crime, seems somehow more guilty. But how do we distinguish between our first defendant and the mother of the cancer patient—or do we? Is driving while tired worse than driving while distracted by grief and worry? If so, why? If a judge gives the mother a lighter sentence, is that based on a belief that her actions were somehow different—less guilty—or based on sympathy? Would the latter be a legitimate basis for mitigating her punishment?

Knowing exactly how to draw the line between like cases and different cases is an art that no judge will ever master once and for all, since each new case potentially raises a different way of understanding similarity and difference. But the need to consider each case in light of the principles of treating like cases alike and different cases differently forces the judge to think about each case not only as a unique

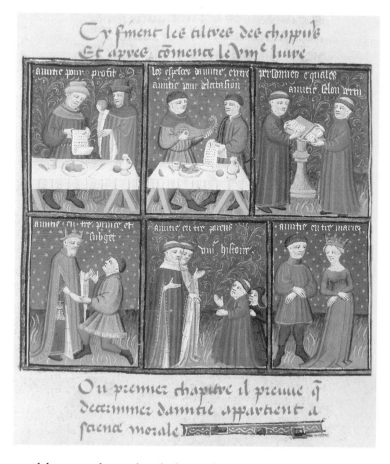

A page from Aristotle's Nicomachean Ethics. *This treatise still influences the modern-day justice system.*

problem to be solved, but also in relation to other cases. Remaining aware of the relationship among cases is one means by which legal officials such as judges can maintain and cultivate a sense of continuity within the life of the law.

The process of sentencing seems, based on the preceding sections, to be a rather complicated effort; but the goal, it would appear, is fairly straightforward: to choose a punishment that fits the crime. This goal—sometimes called "just deserts"—is based on the age-old idea that if a person commits a crime, society itself is the main victim. The only way that society can repair the damage caused by the crime, according to this principle, is if the person who

"Just deserts" might be one goal of punishment, but rehabilitation may be more beneficial to society. Here, inmates learn computer skills to prepare for their eventual release.

committed the crime suffers precisely as much pain as the person caused. Punishing a criminal in this way, then, not only heals society's wounds, but also allows the criminal to "pay his debt" to society and regain membership in it.

Just deserts is an important goal of punishment—but it's by no means the only goal. No matter where you look, you can probably identify examples of punishment that don't conform entirely to this aim. Think, for instance, of a baseball team manager who warns his players that if even one of them starts a fight with an opposing team member, the entire team will be fined. This policy seems unfair on its face: if a player started a brawl and the manager followed through on his threat, several innocent people—people who had not joined the melee—would be punished. But the purpose of the rule is clear: to give players a strong incentive not to fight. Angering one's teammates is likely to be a more unpleasant prospect for most players than simply being fined or suspended for a few games.

The theory behind the manager's strategy is known as deterrence, and it's an important part of the sentencing process as well. Sometimes a judge will impose a sentence that's somewhat more severe than the crime seems to call for—and will explain that the defendant is serving as an example to others of what will happen to them if they engage in the same behavior. Punishment as deterrence can be effective in a number of ways: when enforced, it can dissuade others from committing the same crime; it can prevent a person who's once served as an example from making the same mistake twice; and the mere threat of a harsh punishment can discourage people from committing an offense.

There are limits, of course, on the use of deterrence in sentencing. If judges meted out drastic sentences for every crime they especially wanted to discourage, too many people would receive sentences far out of proportion to their crime. Justice would suffer, and so would our confidence in the legal system: we'd complain that legal officials are more interested in manipulating our behavior than in being fair or just. And we'd lose all sense of perspective on crime. If a judge who hated vandalism decided to begin imposing 10-year prison sentences on graffiti artists, we might soon begin to believe that vandalism is as heinous an offense as robbery or assault with a deadly weapon.

But punishment, by its very nature, usually has a deterrent effect: many of us avoid doing certain things because there's a punishment attached to them, no matter what that punishment may be. Judges may be aware of that effect when they propose a sentence, even as they adhere firmly to the principle of just deserts. In most cases, both of these aims can be met with no conflict.

Deterrence is a practical aim of punishment; it's designed to produce a particular social effect—a reduction in criminal behavior. Another practical goal of punishment is that of incapacitation: in other words, getting dangerous criminals off the streets. There are some crimes—particularly violent ones—that we not only disapprove of, but also fear. Sometimes our main goal in punishing the people who commit those crimes is not to give them what they deserve, nor even to discourage others from doing the same thing; it's to prevent them from finding the opportunity to commit further crimes.

Judges often keep the goal of incapacitation in mind during the sentencing process. Think again of the hit-and-run defendant; suppose that her presentence investigation report read that she'd had two previous arrests for leaving the scene of an accident. Would you be more likely to impose the maximum sentence allowed than you would if those arrests weren't on her record? Probably—and not just because the present crime now looks more serious. You'd begin to see her behavior as part of a pattern, and would be inclined to do what it took to keep her from harming anyone else.

Judges are most likely to impose a sentence guided by the goal of incapacitation on repeat violent offenders. It's a valid aim, but like deterrence, it must not take priority over just deserts. That's because incapacitation is, in a sense, meant to punish people not for what they've done, but for what we fear they will do. Maybe those fears are justified, but the legality of punishing someone for a potential future act is questionable. Judges must make sure that their sentences reflect the seriousness of the crime at hand, not the fear of a crime that's yet to occur.

The fourth and final purpose of punishment is rehabilitation: giving the criminal the tools and opportunity to reform and reenter mainstream life.

In most cases, punishment alone isn't considered rehabilitative, but is supplemented with some activity or program designed to help the individual abandon a life of crime. For example, people convicted of drug-related crimes are often required to participate in drug treatment therapy while in prison or as a condition of their probation. Some prison inmates are taught to read and write, or trained in a career, in the

Most prisoners do not stamp license plates because there is not much use for this skill in the outside world. Prison officials realize that market-able job skills will make the transition to the outside world easier.

hopes that these skills will make the transition to the "outside world" easier for them.

However noble its intent, rehabilitation, like the other purposes of punishment, cannot completely dictate the sentence a judge imposes. Imagine that you're convicted of a crime, and a judge seeks to rehabilitate you. Without the limits of just deserts, what's to stop the judge from sentencing you to a prison term that only ends when you're completely "well"? And who gets to determine when you've reached that point? The goal of rehabilitating criminals can only be pursued within the framework of just deserts—otherwise, doctors, not legal officials, will be in charge of the criminal justice system.

Examining the four purposes of punishment—just deserts, deterrence, incapacitation, and rehabilitation—makes it clear why the sentencing process is often so difficult and wrenching for judges. After all, in determining what sentence to impose, a judge often has to look not only into the past to decide what punishment the defendant deserves; the judge also has to look into the future to decide what that punishment might accomplish. There's seldom anything straightforward about this process.

The delicate balancing act that the judge has to perform in taking these purposes into account explains why even offenders who committed the same crime may receive radically different sentences. One armed robber might get a 20-year sentence; after all, the judge reasons, it's the offender's fourth felony conviction— the robber is beyond rehabilitation and should be prevented from committing even more violent crimes. Another armed robber might receive the minimum sentence plus mandatory drug treatment because the judge thinks there's still a chance for the robber to turn his or her life around, and a long prison term might do more harm than good for the offender and the offender's family.

The decisions that sentencing judges make are seldom easy ones, and they may not always be the right ones. But when they're made with all the relevant facts at hand, and when judges adhere closely to the principles of law that ground the practice of sentencing, those decisions will approach as near as humanly possible to the ideal of justice.

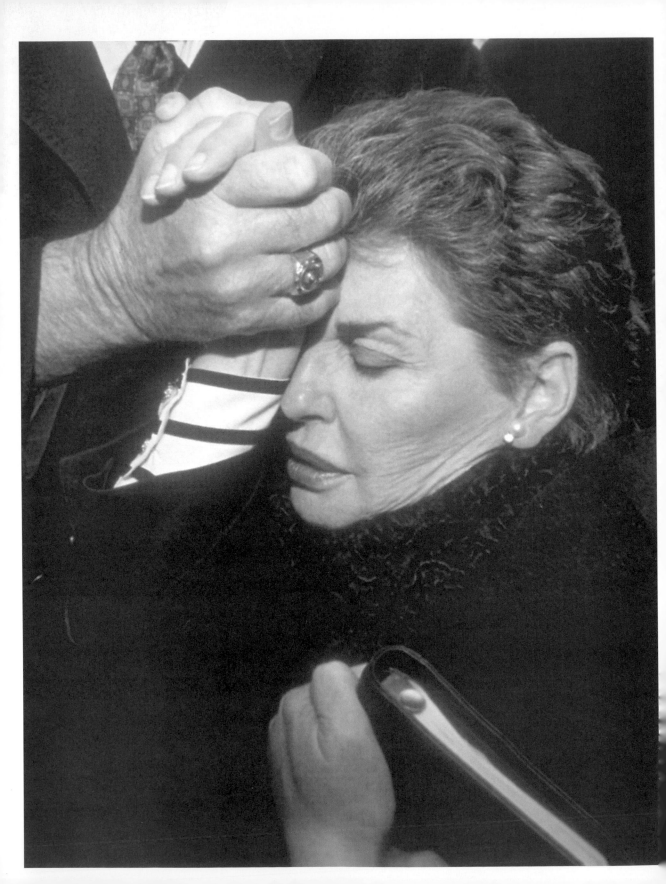

Sentencing White-collar Criminals: The Judge's Dilemma

O n April 15, 1992, Leona Helmsley, formerly the owner of a chain of luxury hotels, went to prison for conspiring to defraud the government of $1.2 million in taxes. Even though she had been indicted four years earlier, the event still made headlines across the nation, and Americans still read them with mixed emotions: they chuckled at the timing (April 15 is tax deadline day) and shook their heads in disbelief at her grand "entrance" (she flew to the prison in a private jet). The Leona Helmsley saga had drawn the public's attention for a number of reasons. For one thing, Helmsley was something of a character, albeit a villainous one: she was ostentatious, brash, and abrasive, and it was said that she treated her employees harshly and with contempt. For another, she had flaunted her crimes as if they were badges of honor: "only the little people pay taxes," she once reportedly boasted.

But the thing that perhaps accounted most for the

Millionaire Leona Helmsley collapses after being ordered to begin her four-year sentence for income tax evasion. Her sentence was to start on April 15, 1992 —tax day.

intense focus on Helmsley's case was the fact that we so seldom see people like her prosecuted for crimes such as those of which she was eventually convicted. Most crimes, of course, don't make the papers or the evening news, and the ones that do are usually violent ones, committed by people whose names we don't recognize and perhaps causing us to fear for our safety or to feel compassion for the victims. This crime was different, and it stirred a different set of feelings about crime and justice. We didn't care much about the details of her crimes—there's nothing salacious or provocative about writing in the wrong numbers on a tax form—but we did care about what happened to her, and about the message that the federal district court judge's sentence would send about her crimes.

Helmsley's tax fraud belongs to a class of crime defined as economic, or "white-collar," meaning that it's nonviolent and usually involves cheating or dishonesty in commercial matters. Her case was not the only one of its kind that graced the front pages of newspapers and magazines during the late 1980s and early 1990s: in the same period, Wall Street players Ivan Boesky and Michael Milken were sentenced to 3 years and 10 years respectively for their roles in illegal insider-trading activity. The aggressive prosecution of major-league white-collar crime during this period was probably not coincidental: the 1980s have been called "the decade of greed," and it was a time during which hostile corporate takeovers and high-stakes stock speculation were taking place with unprecedented frequency and under ethically and legally questionable circumstances. It was not a stretch to see the government's aggressive pursuit of conviction, and the judges' willingness to impose unusually severe sentences, as a not-very-veiled message: high-flying financial shenanigans would no longer be tolerated.

Many people saw justice in the sentences imposed on Helmsley, Boesky, and Milken; others were

Wall Street tycoon Michael Milken was sentenced to 10 years in jail for insider trading violations. He was a major player in the 1980s' "decade of greed."

uncomfortable with the harshness of the terms, especially since their crimes hadn't really hurt anyone in a tangible way. Some pointed out that the average rapist gets off easier than Milken did. This series of cases raised questions in the public mind that many judges have to grapple with on a regular basis: How do we assess the blameworthiness of white-collar criminals? On what basis do we determine the seriousness of the wrongdoing involved? And what theory should we employ in meting out sentences against them?

Judges, when confronted by a case of embezzlement or tax evasion, have a very different sentencing task than they do when they face a case of robbery or mayhem. One important difference is that it's often harder to figure out how much blame the offender really deserves in the crime. A paper trail may have pointed to the individual's guilt; but the question of just how much punishment that guilt warrants depends on factors that the trial or plea agreement may not have established.

Imagine, for instance, that a group of individuals at a firm pled guilty to or were convicted of "cooking the books"—manipulating the figures in the accounting ledgers in order to mislead others about the financial state of the company. It may not be easy to tell who knew what, when, in the course of the crime. The judge may well want to try to figure out which defendants were involved in planning the scheme, and which ones were recruited after the fact or decided to go along with it instead of rocking the boat. The judge may also want to determine the amount of involvement each had in the scheme: Did one give the orders, and the rest just plug in the phony numbers? Does it matter if some of them didn't know for sure that something illegal was going on, but strongly suspected it? Finally, the judge may try to learn what the intent of the various players was. Should it make a difference if some of them were drawing illegal profits strictly out of greed, while one had a gambling addiction to maintain and another was struggling to pay his son's medical bills?

The answer seems to be that all of these distinctions matter, but the evidence may not provide the answers that would allow many of the distinctions to be made. In the end, the judge is likely to try to identify the leaders of the plan and sentence them more severely than the rest. A more difficult set of questions arises when the judge looks at the harm that the crime caused. We—and judges—may have little difficulty identifying this aspect when it comes to violent crimes:

the existence of a harm is uncontroversial, and it may
pose little challenge to determine just how much harm
it was. Some forms of white-collar crime are similarly
transparent when it comes to the crime involved:
insurance scams and pyramid schemes designed to bilk
elderly people out of their life savings, for instance, or
bribes paid to housing inspectors that get landlords out
of making improvements to their buildings, produce
harms that we can see and that tend to outrage us.

For the most part, however, white-collar crime
tends to be different, since often (as in Helmsley's case)
the only victim is the government, or (as in Boesky's
and Milken's cases) the victims might be other
investors, firms, or financial institutions, but the harm
is diffuse and difficult to see as a direct result of the
crime. Moreover, some economic crimes are difficult
for anyone except the financially savvy to follow; we
may be able to glean from the details that there was
illegal intent and illegal behavior, but just what distinguishes it from acceptable activity isn't always entirely
clear to the untrained eye. In the end, we may not feel
the same sense of moral disapproval for someone who
defrauds a corporation that we do for someone who
robs a bank—even if the bank robber physically harms
no one, and gets away with a fraction of the money
that the defrauder did. And judges, to the extent that
they are no more familiar with the ins and outs of the
financial world than most of the rest of us, may also
lack the instinctual perception of the existence of
harm in these cases.

What is often required in these cases is a different
or more expansive definition of harm. In violent
criminal actions, harm is literal and objectively identifiable; in economic crime, however, it may be
abstract and intangible. One way of understanding
the harm that economic crime can cause is to see it as
destructive of public trust. Much white-collar crime
takes place from within institutions that all of us

count on in our daily lives: banks and other financial institutions, governmental agencies, hospitals, schools, and private businesses. The direct harms of those crimes may be difficult to discern, but their cumulative effects are easier to understand. Cheating and dishonesty within the organizations that make up the foundations of our society, especially public bodies, can make us lose faith not only in those organizations, but also in the integrity of society itself.

Looked at this way, the problem of white-collar crime may appear particularly troubling. Most judges take the issue of public trust very seriously; they are likely to remember the political and social crisis that resulted from the Watergate scandal during the Nixon administration, when high officials in the federal government engaged in illegal activities designed to shore up the administration's power. America was profoundly shaken as a result of the Watergate revelations, and its repercussions are still felt in the residual distrust that some feel toward the government. Judges are likely to take this history into account in considering the harm caused by white-collar crime.

Even after assessing the amount of harm and blameworthiness involved in a white-collar offense, a judge may have difficulty finding the right sentence to impose. Some assumptions that underlie the sentencing process in common criminal cases often don't apply. For example, the white-collar criminal is very unlikely to pose a danger to public safety or order, so it may be difficult to justify a prison sentence over a fine or restitution. Moreover, most people convicted of white-collar offenses have no prior record, and therefore, all else being equal, may seem to deserve probation rather than prison. Finally, it may be difficult to make an argument that a prison sentence would serve to reform or rehabilitate the white-collar criminal: economic crimes are generally motivated by greed or

Many Americans lost faith in government and society because of the Watergate scandal during the Nixon administration. Judges sometimes remember Watergate and other scandals as they decide the sentences of white-collar criminals.

temptation, which unfortunately are virtually universal human traits. If an individual convicted of a white-collar crime seems remorseful and appears free of socially deviant qualities that might require rehabilitation, incarcerating her or him might seem wasteful and unlikely to serve any identifiable purpose.

If, on balance, a white-collar offender seems to deserve a fine rather than a prison term, a judge may nonetheless hesitate to impose such a sentence. One reason is that many—though by no means all—white-collar criminals have deep pockets, and may be able to withstand such a punishment without breaking stride. For an offender who's not at all repentant, the fine may be viewed merely as a cost of doing business, and may not prevent future criminal activity. Another reason is that the judge may be afraid of appearing too lenient toward white-collar criminals. After all, in this country, judges are more likely to share similar socioeconomic backgrounds and cultural values with white-collar offenders, who tend to come from middle- and upper-middle-class sectors of society. A judge may not have much in common with drug dealers, muggers, or prostitutes. A judge who imposes an economic sentence for a white-collar crime will be vulnerable to accusations of favoritism—or, in any event, a judge may fear that vulnerability. For either of these reasons, then, a judge might feel some pressure to impose a prison sentence, despite misgivings about its likely effectiveness, practicality, or suitability.

A third reason that a judge might find a harsher sanction appropriate is the reason that was imputed to the judges who sentenced Helmsley, Boesky, and Milken: the desire to "send a message" that white-collar crime is just as heinous, in the eyes of the law, as malicious violent crime. A judge thus would embrace a deterrent theory of punishment; the object of the deterrence, however, is not the criminal, but rather other potential violators of the same law. Realistically, such a message is likely to ring loud and clear: don't count on breaking the law and getting away with it. The justice of such a tactic, however, is dubious. Is it fair to make an example of someone in this way? Is it good judicial practice to use people as means to an end, even if that end is the admittedly laudable one of deterring other people from committing crimes?

The dilemma that the white-collar criminal poses for the sentencing judge may never be overcome. Balancing the need to make the punishment fit the offense with the desire to express condemnation of economic crime may never result in a completely palatable compromise. Part of the problem, however, may be in the limited choice that judges may have: a fine or imprisonment. Alternative sentencing may provide a more satisfying solution to the difficulty. An example that some judges have put into practice is sentencing landlords convicted of repeatedly violating housing codes to live in their own run-down properties. Such a sentence, when combined with a fine and restitution to anyone injured as a result of unsafe conditions in the building, may serve a range of punishment purposes: not only would it likely result in the landlord's making a concerted effort to improve conditions, but it may also make other landlords more scrupulous about making repairs. Moreover, it provides a kind of "poetic justice" that's remarkably satisfying, and—particularly in the realm of white-collar crime—regrettably rare.

SENTENCING REFORM, PART ONE: THE RISE AND FALL OF THE REHABILITATIVE SENTENCE

Americans have always had ambivalent feelings about crime and punishment. As a group, we tend to waver between a stern, punitive attitude toward criminal behavior on one hand, and the suspicion that punishment may not always be the best or most appropriate response to some crimes on the other. We argue among ourselves about the purposes of punishment, the effectiveness of certain kinds of sentences, and the justice and fairness of the system in how it treats people convicted of crimes. We may agree, in the end, that punishment is necessary in human society—but we continue to disagree heatedly about what punishment, how to punish, and why.

Despite our long history of debate on the very meaning of punishing criminals, for a period of nearly 100 years our nation pursued a penal policy that was, in principle, single-minded in its goal: wherever possible, to rehabilitate criminal offenders. This chapter explores

Americans agree that punishment is necessary but continue to disagree heatedly about what punishment, how to punish, and why.

the ways in which rehabilitation was embraced as an ideal; the changes adopted by both courts and legislatures in making rehabilitation a priority in sentencing; the sentencing strategies—particularly the indeterminate sentence and the therapeutic sentence—that were intended to make rehabilitation possible; and the social changes and criticisms that have led to the gradual abandonment both of rehabilitation as a primary goal of punishment, and of sentencing schemes that were designed to promote rehabilitation.

If you're familiar with stories about the Salem witch trials of the 17th century, or the use of public beating and humiliation to punish wrongdoers in colonial America, you know that we have not always thought about punishment primarily as a means of reforming the criminal. It's true that some of these early punishments might have been intended to "reform" the criminal, in the sense that it was hoped that those who once endured harsh treatment at the hands of the state might be persuaded to follow a straighter path in the future. However, most of the sentences that judges meted out in the colonial years and the early decades of democracy were designed with retribution—that is, vengeance—in mind. The criminal was judged to have injured not only the victim, if there was one, but also the community itself. Crime disturbed public safety and order, but also was considered sinful and for this reason threatened the community's moral stability. It was this harm that the sentence was meant to repay: an eye for an eye, a tooth for a tooth.

It was not unusual during this period for convicted wrongdoers to receive a sentence of banishment. Such a sentence was an expression of the community's belief that the criminal had stepped over a critical line: because of the seriousness of the offense, or because the criminal had committed enough prior offenses to be considered a lost cause, the offender was viewed as

having been effectively placed outside the bounds of the community. Banishment was not only final, it was serious: once banished, a person would have trouble being accepted into another community and would be forced to fend for himself or herself. Survival was a matter of luck and resourcefulness.

It was not until the middle of the 19th century that this mostly retributive approach to sentencing began to change. Largely as a result of Enlightenment ideas imported from Europe, Americans began to think about crime and punishment in new and more rational ways. Rather than regarding criminals as morally corrupt or sinful, people started to see them as having a weakness of character for which punishment could

Some early judges meted out punishment with retribution or vengeance in mind. The prisoners at Old Newgate Prison were forced to work in the prison's copper mines. This 18th-century prison is now a Connecticut tourist attraction.

be a remedy. The penitentiary—a relatively recent invention—was in a sense the physical incarnation of this idea: people came to believe that putting a convicted criminal in prison was a way not just of avenging the offense or of protecting the community against a potentially dangerous individual, but also of allowing the criminal to reflect upon his or her crimes in solitude and, ideally, to come to regret them. The notion contained in the idea of the "penitentiary"— that it was a place where offenders would become penitent, or remorseful, and thus willing to leave behind their evil ways—was originally grounded in the Christian belief in the importance of repenting one's sins. However, the penitentiary also lent itself well to the new, less outwardly religious belief that even hardened criminals could become reformed in the penitentiary context.

What was the reasoning behind the 19th-century belief that the penitentiary could rehabilitate offenders? One reason was that people believed that criminals were "created" by their surroundings: some were the products of poor parenting, while others were corrupted by their morally degenerate associates, and still others had been brought low by the effects of excessive drinking—and for some, it was some combination of the three. During this period there was both a tremendous concern with issues of social deviancy, and a powerful new belief that deviant behavior could be corrected. Penitentiaries made it possible to remove criminals from their "unhealthy" environments and tendencies, and to instill in them new habits of discipline and order. This was accomplished in a variety of ways: first, imprisoned convicts had to abide by strict timetables that dictated when they awoke and went to bed, when they ate, and when they worked or studied. Second, work and study themselves were viewed as rehabilitative, since many people assumed that idleness and lack of schooling could lead the way to criminal habits. Most penitentiary inmates found the Bible at the top of their required reading list.

Another reason that the penitentiary was seen as such an effective rehabilitative tool was that it seemed to lend itself so well to the enduring notion that the punishment should fit the crime. The influence of rational ideas about crime, punishment, and justice made both officials and the public at large sensitive to the problems associated with other forms of punishment, such as public humiliation, flogging, and capital punishment. Such means of punishment often seemed harsher than the crime warranted, or at any rate were difficult to match exactly to the severity of the crime: how many lashes with a whip does a pickpocket deserve? Not only was it impossible to determine with any precision just how much suffering such a punishment produced; but it also became clear that some offenders were thicker-skinned than others, and thus that the same punishment would not affect two wrongdoers in the same way. These dilemmas gnawed at the reform-minded. The penitentiary, however, provided an ingenious solution: the ability to link a particular offense to a specific term behind bars made the punishment seem less arbitrary and more rational. Since time passed at the same rate for everyone, it was possible in theory to determine equitable, uniform, and fair sentences for each offender.

Another reason—rather distinct from, if not in conflict with, the last—was the increasingly popular belief that the punishment should fit not only the crime, but the criminal as well. If punishment was in fact meant to rehabilitate the offender, it was crucial to pay attention not only to the crime, but also to all the factors that might have contributed to the criminal behavior. That meant investigating the offender's childhood, family background, schooling, marital history, prior record, friends and associates, employment history, and even attitude: was the offender remorseful,

Eastern State Penitentiary in Philadelphia, considered the first modern prison, became a model for prisons throughout the world. Prisoners were kept in solitary confinement and expected to read the Bible, work, and reflect on their crimes.

passive, angry, stubborn? Taking these facts into account, a judge could prescribe a sentence that would not only measure up to the offense, but also enable those administering that sentence to take steps toward counteracting the negative life influences of the offender and toward molding him or her into a potentially productive and valuable member of society. The beauty of the penitentiary, in the eyes of 19th-century penal reformers, was that it could encompass the various goals of punishment, including rehabilitation. A judge could design a sentence that took into consideration how long it might take to reform the offender, as well as the various techniques that might be used to bring about that reform. For example, an inmate who had never gone to school or held a job might be taught a trade, taught to read and write, and confined for long enough to develop habits of hard work and obedience.

A difficult question soon arose, however. If rehabilitation was the primary object of punishment, how much sense did it make to determine in advance the length of the sentence? In doing so, a judge would be making merely an educated guess as to how much time it would take for a criminal to shed his or her bad habits and to develop good ones. Recognizing this, many jurisdictions began adopting an indeterminate sentencing scheme toward the end of the 19th century. By 1907, it was possible for Eugene Smith, president of the Prison Association of New York, to announce that the retributive theory of punishment had been "thoroughly discredited," and to state that "[t]he indeterminate sentence is so logically reasonable, so easy of comprehension and so commends itself to common intelligence, that it has, within a few years, secured wide adoption. It is now firmly incorporated in the penal systems of about one-third of the states of the union, comprising those of the greatest power and influence. There is no longer need of argument in support of the indeterminate sentence."

Indeterminate sentences soon became even more widespread, becoming the primary sentencing method throughout the nation. But not every state or local criminal justice system employed indeterminate sentencing in precisely the same way. Most systems had a penal code that defined for each class of felony and misdemeanor a minimum sentence, a maximum sentence, both, or, increasingly, just a maximum. The prescribed sentencing range could involve a fine, imprisonment, or both. Within the generally broad range, the judge was usually granted wide discretion to consider whatever facts were at hand in imposing sentence. A judge might impose a more limited term than the one allowed by the penal code, or alternatively might allow the range prescribed by the code to stand. In many jurisdictions, when imprisonment was the sentence imposed, it was understood that the offender would serve at least one-third of the maximum term prescribed by the judge, but no more than two-thirds of that maximum.

If the judge didn't mete out a fixed sentence, how were penitentiary and jail administrators supposed to know when to let the offender out? The answer became the parole board, a group of criminal justice officials and social scientists appointed by the government, charged with the duty of evaluating the inmate's fitness for release. Parole officials today look at a wide variety of evidence, among which the inmate's behavior while incarcerated is of primary importance. Has the inmate stayed away from fights with other inmates and conflicts with guards? Has the inmate demonstrated a willing attitude toward the requirements of life behind bars, whether those included work in prison industry, participation in drug or alcohol treatment, or studying toward a high school equivalency degree? Does the inmate express remorse for her or his crimes and appear to be well prepared to reenter the outside world as a productive and trustworthy member of society? The parole board also looks at the situation that awaits the inmate on the outside. Does the inmate have opportunities for gainful employment? What is the inmate's family situation? Will the inmate be able to avoid the negative influences and circumstances that originally led to criminal activity?

At a predesignated point during the inmate's term,

she or he will go before the board, answering questions and attempting to convince the board members of her or his readiness to leave prison. If they disagree, the inmate will continue serving the sentence until a set period of time passes and the inmate is again eligible for parole. If they believe that the inmate is reformed, the inmate will be released; usually, however, as conditions of the parole, the inmate will be subject to a number of limitations on his or her freedom. For example, the inmate may not be able to associate with other convicted felons, or may be required to attend drug or alcohol treatment or support groups, or may

Howard Unruh gunned down 13 people in his Camden, New Jersey, neighborhood in 1947. Officials are not sure if Unruh has been rehabilitated. They have reviewed the case periodically and have denied his repeated requests for less-secure incarceration.

be barred from taking certain kinds of employment (a convicted embezzler, for instance, may not be able to hold a job that requires handling money), or may be required to make restitution to victims, or may have to live in a "halfway house" for a set period of time, during which the inmate's comings and goings are strictly controlled.

The upshot of the indeterminate sentence is that the job of sentencing is shared between the judge and the parole board. What we may idealize as a process by which a judge looks at offenders and their crimes, and comes up with sentences that comport most closely with standards of fairness and justice, actually has become something far more complicated. Different factors now come into play; sentencing during the course of the 20th century became an increasingly "scientific" undertaking, involving sociological and criminological theories of deviance, psychological studies of the causes of antisocial behavior, and analysis of the likelihood that people from various backgrounds will revert to criminal activity once released from jail or prison. Judges, however, for the most part have not quarreled with dividing their sentencing responsibilities with a parole board. This may be in large part because they have tended to share the commonly held belief that the main purpose of punishment should be rehabilitation, and that the officials who have the best understanding of how best to effect reform should be in charge of determining the details of the sentence.

In some cases, however, the judge will impose a more defined sentence, and one that diverges from the typical choice between a fine and imprisonment. Judges may do this for a variety of reasons, but foremost among them is the sentiment—which gained force during the last half of the 20th century—that traditional methods of punishment weren't effective enough in rehabilitating offenders. Another reason was that many judges came to believe that too much attention was being focused on the criminal at the expense of the crime's victim. These two factors, while they seem to stand in contradiction to one another, may not in fact be so divergent: some judges operate on the theory that if a criminal is given the opportunity to make amends to the victim, that experience itself can have a rehabilitative impact. Whatever the impetus, a lack of faith in conventional sentences has prompted judges to opt for alternative and occasionally even innovative sentences.

We may not think of probation as a particularly creative sentence, but since the mid-19th century it's been by far the most established alternative sentence in use. Particularly for first-time offenders, a term of probation is actually the sentence a judge is most likely to impose. Probation is generally given in lieu of a possible jail sentence or fine (although a fine may be imposed in conjunction with probation), and may involve a number of conditions: a person on probation may be required to submit to regular drug tests, attend anger management classes, or attend job training sessions.

One reason judges may impose probation instead of another possible sentence is mercy: it may seem unreasonable or cruel to put someone behind bars because of a stupid mistake the person is not likely to repeat, or because of a crime stemming from circumstances beyond the person's control (for example, a recently laid-off worker who steals from a grocery store to feed his family). Another reason is a concern for rehabilitation: a stint behind bars may do little good for someone with a substance abuse or mental health problem; probation conditioned on seeking treatment might be more sensible in some circumstances. A third reason is sheer pragmatics: jail and prison overcrowding have made it impractical in some jurisdictions to incarcerate any but the most violent offenders.

Furthermore, if a judge sees that a convicted criminal is the sole source of support for his or her family, or if the judge believes that the criminal should pay restitution to the victim, the judge may decide to give the criminal probation so that he or she can continue to earn money to meet these financial obligations.

Restitution is a frequently imposed alternative sentence. While it may seem like a sentence that's best suited to offenders with ample financial resources, it's not uncommon for a judge to sentence a poor offender to pay the victim back for damages or hospital bills in small installments. One judge, for instance, sentenced a man convicted of several assault and weapons charges to 19 years' probation, during which time he was required to pay his victim (who was permanently blinded) $25 per week. The victim would thus receive a total of nearly $25,000; and the offender, who had previously been employed only irregularly, was forced to find steady work—thus bringing a rehabilitative element to the sentence. Some suggest an added rehabilitative aspect of restitution: offenders, by making their victims "whole" again, recognize both the harm that their actions caused and their capacity for constructive action as well.

Other common alternative sentences include commitment to a psychiatric or drug and alcohol treatment facility and performance of community service. In the latter case, a judge may try to impose a sentence that's particularly well suited to the crime: for instance, a person convicted of vandalism may be sentenced to several consecutive weekends of cleaning graffiti from public buildings, or someone who caused an injury while driving drunk may have to speak to groups of grade school students about the dangers of drug and alcohol abuse. The idea, clearly, is to kill two birds with one stone: to allow the individual to make up for the crime, and to force the individual to reflect upon its consequences on an up-close-and-personal basis.

A judge may try to impose a sentence that's particularly well suited to the crime. A person convicted of vandalism may be sentenced to several consecutive weekends of cleaning graffiti from public buildings.

The indeterminate sentence and other sentencing schemes based on a theory of rehabilitation have had a long run in the American criminal justice system. Up until relatively recently, they were accepted without much question, since the rehabilitative ideal remained dominant across society. Beginning in the 1970s, however, critics of rehabilitative sentencing, and particularly of the indeterminate sentence, started to make themselves heard.

One voice of protest was that of a prisoners' rights movement that had emerged in various parts of the country. Its advocates pointed to the drastic limitation of civil rights that rehabilitative sentencing could justify. In principle, the main factor in the length of a person's sentence was whether the inmate appeared to a parole board to have been reformed. That meant that a convicted rapist could be released after a year in prison—assuming he made a good impression during his parole hearing—while someone who forged a check might be kept behind bars for five years if parole officials weren't convinced that the offender had mended her or his ways. Unfortunately, sentences such as these are hardly unheard of under an indeterminate sentencing regime, and they highlight a significant problem: inmates may figure out what parole boards want to hear and go through the motions of having been "cured," whether or not they have been—or, for that matter, whether they were "sick" in the first place.

Prisoners' rights advocates also noted that parole could be used both to manipulate and to punish inmates who participated in actions prison officials disapproved of—such as helping other prisoners with their legal appeals or participating in radical political organizations. The question of just how much power the parole board should have, and how it used its power, became central to the question of whether indeterminate sentencing should be retained.

Therapeutic sentencing in general came under similar scrutiny. While it might be laudable to help an offender avoid prison in some cases, some alternative sentences make matters worse and some seem downright questionable. Is it acceptable, some ask, for a judge to require a convicted shoplifter to wear a sign that reads "shoplifter" in public for a fixed period of time? Is it appropriate to require an offender to meet with the victim to apologize—a meeting that the victim might dread as much as, if not more than, the offender? Furthermore, if a person is committed to a psychiatric facility instead of to prison, who then gets to decide when she or he should be released? Some critics point to the problem of criminals who are regarded as "sick" and prescribed treatment yet aren't

extended the same legal protections as those who are placed in a jail cell, since presumably sick people don't need to be protected from those who seek to cure them. The potential for the abuse of civil rights in the name of rehabilitation looms large.

At the same time that objections to rehabilitative sentencing issued from champions of civil rights, other objections began to come from a very different source: law-and-order advocates who believed that indeterminate and alternative sentencing were too soft on crime. The indeterminate sentence, they argued, made it too easy for criminals to escape the long prison terms they deserved and to get back on the street,

Dale Whipple (second from the right) a convicted and paroled murderer, joins hands before a meal with fellow halfway house residents. Critics have assailed indeterminate sentencing schemes that allow such violent offenders to be released into the community after serving only a fraction of the maximum sentence.

once again posing a threat to law-abiding citizens. How, they asked, were Americans supposed to trust the criminal justice system, when a murderer could be sentenced to 25 years in prison and yet could go free after just 6 years?

Likewise, the concern with lax treatment of criminals extended to judges who were too willing to extend probation and suspended sentences to offenders, or to impose sentences that fell short in severity of what seemed to be called for. It was almost impossible to ensure that judges were fulfilling their mandate to "do justice"—which, for many, meant to make sure that criminals were not being coddled. The objection to the amount of discretion that judges could employ was joined by others, many of whom were not so much worried that criminals were getting off with a slap on the wrist as concerned that there was no consistency in the sentences meted out to similar offenders for similar crimes. When judges are allowed to impose whatever sentence they feel is just, the end product turns out to be a certain amount of disparity. Many worried that such disparity has the potential to create cynicism and a loss of faith in the system, that Americans may eventually come to believe that criminal justice is arbitrary and biased. And, given the evidence, such a belief might have been difficult to dispute.

These critics, coming as they did from the political left and right, certainly had different views on crime and criminals. Prisoners' rights activists sympathized more with offenders and believed that rehabilitative sentencing had the power to oppress and manipulate them unjustly. Law-and-order proponents, on the other hand, focused not on the rights of the offender but on the values of legal authority and public order. Both groups, however, found fault with the same aspect of the criminal justice system: too much judicial discretion.

By the 1980s, the controversy surrounding rehabilitative sentencing had come to a head. Battles raged among lawyers, judges, legislators, scholars, activists, and families sitting at the dinner table. What might the solution be to the crisis in sentencing? Many states had already found the answer: their legislatures had passed "truth in sentencing" laws, established independent sentencing commissions, and embraced sentencing guidelines that took most of the guesswork—and the discretion—out of judges' hands. The federal government soon took similar steps. The following chapter explores some of the changes that grew out of the increasing public discontent with indeterminate and alternative sentencing—and that sounded the death knell of the rehabilitative ideal in America.

Sentencing Reform, Part Two: Limits on Judicial Discretion

In 1995, a 24-year-old former honor roll student, Kemba Smith, was sent to federal prison for a 24-year term. Her crimes? Conspiring to sell cocaine, money laundering, and lying to federal authorities. These offenses sound serious, and might seem to merit the severe punishment that the federal judge handed down. The facts of the case, however, caused many observers to question whether such a long prison term was really called for.

While a sophomore in college, Kemba Smith became involved with a man several years her senior. That man, Peter Michael Hall, was the leader of a violent drug ring that had been operating near Smith's college for over a year before the two met. In the course of their relationship, Hall beat Smith and allegedly threatened her life and the lives of her family members if she didn't do what he said. He convinced Smith to smuggle guns and money for him across state lines. After law enforcement officials began seeking

Because of federal mandatory drug sentencing laws, Kemba Smith (whose parents and young son are seen here at the podium during a rally) was sent to federal prison for a 24-year term. She was not a drug dealer but had lied and refused to cooperate with law enforcement officers.

Hall, Smith lied to federal authorities about her involvement with Hall and his drug ring; she helped him dispose of evidence of his crimes, including guns; she accompanied him as he evaded authorities; and she refused to cooperate with federal agents' attempts to track Hall down.

When, after Hall was shot and killed by an unknown assailant, Smith finally turned herself in and tried to cooperate, it was too little, too late. Her previous efforts to protect Hall made the prosecutor and the judge unsympathetic with her hopes for leniency. Smith pled guilty to money laundering, making false statements to federal agents, and conspiring to distribute crack cocaine, in the hope that her plea and the fact that Hall had abused her would give the judge reason to go easy on her. Instead, U.S. district court judge Richard Kellam pronounced a sentence that would have kept Smith behind bars until the child she had with Hall was a grown man, had that sentence not later been commuted.

Kemba Smith's case is a complicated one. Whether she helped Hall mostly because she feared him, or because she was entranced by the money and power that he commanded, or simply because she loved him will never be known for sure. Few would deny that she made a number of grave mistakes and should have cooperated with the authorities from the beginning, but her passive participation in Hall's operation—she never even touched any of the drugs that Hall's organization sold—seems hardly to warrant the harsh sentence she received. One thing, however, is clear: Smith would never have received such a sentence—longer by several years than the average sentence for a convicted murderer—were it not for the strict mandatory minimum sentences for drug offenses dictated by federal law.

The United States has clear and severe guidelines for how drug offenders ought to be punished. These guidelines in their current form were created as provisions of the 1986 Anti-Drug Abuse Act and the 1988 Omnibus

Anti-Drug Abuse Act. Throughout the 1980s, Americans worried a great deal about the dangers of illegal drugs, and many believed that an all-out "war on drugs" was the best solution to the threat that they posed. Legislators believed that the arsenal in that war should include laws that made sentences for drug crimes hard and inflexible. Such laws, they reasoned, would provide a strong deterrent against using and selling illegal drugs. These laws imposed baseline limits on the punishments that judges could assign to convicted drug offenders, depending on the charge and the kind and amount of drugs involved.

Mandatory minimums for drug crime had existed before the 1980s laws—in the 1950s, the Congress passed laws that put first-time drug offenders in prison for 10 years, and gave two-time losers 20-year sentences—but these new federal guidelines were harsher than anything that had come before. And, as Smith learned, these mandatory minimums are not flexible. When she pled guilty to conspiring to distribute crack cocaine, the amount she was charged with conspiring to sell was 255 kilograms—the entire amount that the federal government thought that Hall's organization had sold—even though Smith hadn't even met Hall at the time some of those drugs were sold. That amount of crack was more than enough to trigger an automatic sentence of 20 years, despite the fact that Smith had never before been in trouble with the law and hadn't participated directly in selling drugs.

Kemba Smith's sentence was commuted by President Clinton in December 2000, so she served just 6 years of her 24-year term. Her case, however, drew the attention of critics of mandatory minimum sentences, who say that it's just this sort of case that demonstrates the flaws of inflexible sentencing schemes. These critics argue that when judges are forced to sentence defendants based upon a predefined set of facts—which drug, how much, and what the defendant did with it—and aren't allowed to consider mitigating factors such as the defendant's state of mind, her otherwise clean record, and her relatively limited involvement in the crime, unjust and disproportionate sentences are the result. What's more, they point out, prisons are filling up with nonviolent offenders like Smith. Is this, they ask, the best use of government money and resources?

Mandatory minimum sentences for federal drug offenders—as well as for offenders who use guns in the course of their crime—are only one instance of a wide array of controls that have been placed on judges' ability to use discretion in sentencing. One of the best known, and most controversial, of recent moves toward reducing the amount of discretion judges can use in sentencing are the "three-strikes-and-you're-out" laws. These laws, the first of which was passed in California in 1994, were designed to thwart career criminals—those who commit many crimes and who aren't deterred or rehabilitated by prison or jail. Three-strikes laws take a variety of forms, but most of them specify that a second felony conviction will earn a defendant a sentence double that of a first conviction for the same crime—and a person convicted of a third felony will draw a sentence of at least 25 years.

The logic behind three-strikes laws is compelling. If a convicted felon continues to commit serious crimes after he or she has been let out of prison, isn't it in the best interest of the public to keep that person behind bars to prevent her or him from victimizing others? This reasoning involves understanding punishment as a way of incapacitating clearly dangerous individuals. The appeal of this reasoning became powerful after the arrest of Richard Allen Davis for the abduction and murder of 12-year-old Polly Klaas. Davis was the essence of a career criminal: he'd been arrested dozens of times during the course of his life and had spent many years in jail or prison on various charges. It was apparent to many that if three-strikes laws had been

in effect earlier, Davis would still have been safely behind bars and would never have had the opportunity to kidnap Klaas from her Petaluma, California, home and murder her in cold blood. It was in larger part Klaas's tragic—and, in the eyes of many, preventable—death that led to the passage of the first three-strikes law.

From the beginning, however, the three-strikes laws posed problems and drew objections, both ethical and practical. From the perspective of ethics, judges argued that the prescribed sentences prevented them from exercising the discretion that each defendant deserved —and that justice demanded. Some people thought that three strikes was a form of double jeopardy—that is, that it penalized people for old crimes for which

Richard Allen Davis was charged with the abduction and murder of 12-year-old Polly Klaas. A career criminal, Davis would probably have been in jail if three-strikes laws had been in effect earlier, thus preventing his crime.

Polly Klaas's tragic abduction and murder helped put a human face on three-strikes legislation, but critics say the laws are unfair to nonviolent felons and will lead to even-greater prison overcrowding.

they'd already been tried, convicted, and punished. Others called attention to the fact that using punishment to incapacitate an offender was, in essence, punishment for crimes as yet uncommitted, on the presumption that—as a career criminal—she or he probably will commit them. For all of these reasons, critics argued, three-strikes laws may not only be unfair, but may also violate the constitutionally protected rights of criminal defendants.

Besides ethical concerns, critics charged that

three-strikes laws would pose practical problems. Many worried that sympathetic juries would refuse to convict defendants if they knew that a guilty verdict would put the defendant behind bars for 25 years or more. And still others were concerned that three-strikes would lead to major prison overcrowding and that nonviolent felons would bear the burden of increased sentences as much as violent offenders would.

Some of these fears were soon realized. A case that stimulated a national debate about three-strikes laws was that of Jerry Williams, a five-time felon whose conviction in March 1995 triggered a 25-years-to-life sentence. Williams was no choirboy: he'd been arrested 13 times in his life for crimes that included vandalism, burglary, and drug possession. But the crime that made him eligible for three strikes—stealing a slice of pepperoni pizza on a dare—was hardly what the champions of the California law had in mind.

Some people still approved of the sentence: however petty the crime, they argued, it demonstrated beyond a doubt that Williams was a repeat offender, incapable of being reformed. But the California Supreme Court ruled in 1996 that the three-strikes law in its current form was too drastic; sentencing judges needed the authority to weigh factors in a case like Williams's, rather than having to follow the legislature's guidelines blindly. As a result, Williams's case was sent back to superior court judge Donald Pitts, the judge who originally sentenced him. Pitts considered the crime at issue and the defendant's prior record, and reduced the notorious pizza thief's prison term to six years.

In the wake of California's struggle, other states have designed statutes that have limited the applicability of their three-strikes laws. For example, Arizona adopted a law that subjects only violent repeat offenders to progressively harsher penalties. But the popularity of three-strikes legislation, whatever forms it takes, sadly reflects a commonly held belief: that judicial discretion alone isn't sufficient to ensure justice—and that, in some cases, that discretion can actually impede justice.

This belief is revealed in other developments as well. One of the most striking examples of this apparent lack of faith in judicial discretion is the creation of sentencing commissions by the federal government and by a growing number of state governments. The purpose of sentencing commissions is to establish guidelines for judges to apply in sentencing criminals. These guidelines tell judges what factors to consider when imposing sentences, and dictate the precise weight that each of those factors should carry in the judge's decisions.

For instance, suppose you're a judge charged with sentencing a man found guilty of bank robbery. In coming up with the appropriate sentence, you must ask a number of questions about the offense as well as the offender: How much money was taken? Was a gun involved? Was anybody harmed? Does the robber have any prior convictions? Did the robber evade arrest? You'd then consult the chart drawn up by the sentencing commission to determine, based on the answers to those questions, what type and length of sentence to impose.

Maybe you're dissatisfied with the figure that emerges from your calculations; you think that the man's unusual situation—a gambling addiction, per- haps, or an ailing spouse—should lessen the severity of his sentence. You could impose a milder sentence than the one the guidelines dictate, but you'd also be required to explain your decision in writing. Even with that justification, any departure from the guidelines makes your sentence more vulnerable to appeal: if your sentence is lower than the guidelines call for, the prosecutor may challenge your decision; if it's higher, the defendant may take his case to a higher court.

What's the purpose of sentencing guidelines? They seem, on the surface, to duplicate the work that judges are already doing when they impose a sentence. They also have the power to limit the judge's use of discretion. Even if a judge may have a valid or compelling reason to depart from the guidelines, he or she may decide not to for fear that the sentence will be rejected on appeal. Not surprisingly, most judges dislike guidelines. A 1994 poll of district judges found that 86.4 percent support changing sentencing rules to increase the judge's discretion. J. Lawrence Irving, a respected federal judge, resigned in 1990, saying that "the main reason has to do with the sentencing guidelines. . . . Before, we had unlimited discretion in fashioning sentences to fit individual cases. But the guidelines have taken away from judges all such discretion."

Yet some would argue that the "unlimited discretion" that Irving referred to is precisely what makes the guidelines so necessary. One of the primary reasons guidelines were developed was to combat the problem of sentence disparity, the very different sentences judges meted out to similar defendants convicted of similar crimes. Beginning as early as 1914, studies of the sentencing practices of judges have consistently shown remarkable variation in how, and how much, different judges sentence. In a 1974 experiment, 50 district court judges were each given the same 20 hypothetical pre-sentencing reports and were asked what sentences they would impose. The differences were significant, even dramatic: one case drew both a 3-year sentence and a 20-year sentence; in another case, one judge meted out a 3-year term and another judge imposed a suspended sentence. Perhaps even more troubling, studies have shown that nonwhite defendants tend to draw longer sentences than white defendants do. Given sentence disparity, it would appear that judges' discretion should be limited in the interest of justice and fairness.

Another reason that sentencing guidelines were developed was to move toward the ideal of "truth in sentencing." One of the problems with the

President Clinton signs a crime bill into law as others, including Polly Klaas's father, Marc, look on. Legislators create sentencing guidelines, but most judges believe that guidelines take away their discretion and authority.

indeterminate sentencing system is that in it people seldom serve more than a fraction of the maximum term imposed by the judge. Prison officials and parole boards, not judges, have the final say in how long an individual will remain behind bars. The legislatures that create sentencing commissions are worried that misleading sentences give citizens reason to distrust government and the law. Most sentencing commissions eliminate parole entirely, thereby ensuring that every prisoner serves the time (minus a small proportion for good behavior) that the judge imposes.

The present conflict over sentencing boils down to a single question: which is more likely to result in justice—a system that relies on a limited set of guidelines, or one that rests on the discretion of individual judges? The answer is far from clear. We'd like to be able to ensure that the sentencing process is free from the biases, blind spots, and inconsistencies of judges, and it may seem that guidelines are the best solution, but the guidelines, as well researched and carefully thought out as they may be, can have blind spots of their own. The U.S. Sentencing Commission, in outlining its approach, admitted that its efforts to account for all relevant factors in constructing the guidelines were limited by practical considerations. "A sentencing system tailored to fit every conceivable wrinkle of each case," the commission said, "would quickly become unworkable and seriously compromise the certainty of punishment and its deterrent effect. . . . The Commission had to balance the comparative virtues and vices of broad, simple categorization and detailed, complex subcategorization, and within the constraints established by that balance, minimize the discretionary powers of the sentencing court. Any system will, to a degree, enjoy the benefits and suffer from the drawbacks of each approach." Sentencing commissions have to restrict the range of factors that the guidelines can take into account, or the decision process would take so long that no one would ever get sentenced! But judges, however arbitrary their decisions may sometimes seem, are not bound by these same limitations. They can weigh a broad array of considerations and may even use subjective data—a gut feeling, for example—to make their decisions.

We may like the fact that judges have so many tools at their disposal in the sentencing process, but we dislike the flip side of that coin: that they also can be arbitrary, biased, and just plain wrong in their decisions. Is there a way to combine the best qualities of judicial discretion—its broad scope, its flexibility, its ability to recognize the uniqueness of every defendant, its capacity for mercy—with those of sentencing guidelines: evenhandedness, predictability, clarity?

THE FUTURE
OF SENTENCING

In September 1997, district court judge Morris E. Lasker was invited to speak before the Symposium on Sentencing Guidelines, a group jointly organized by Senator Edward Kennedy and Representative John Conyers. The purpose of the symposium was to inquire into whether federal sentencing guidelines were working as planned, and whether any unforeseen consequences had arisen from the guidelines. This, in part, is what Judge Lasker had to say:

A prisoner phones for bail money after learning he is to be released from the overcrowded New York City jail system as a result of an order from Judge Morris Lasker. Judge Lasker has been a critic of mandatory sentencing laws and prison overcrowding.

> Prior to the passage of the Sentencing Reform Act of 1984, which created the Sentencing Guidelines Commission, I testified both before the House and Senate favoring enactment of the legislation. I did so because I believed that the then existing system of sentencing, which gave judges nearly unlimited discretion in imposing sentences, resulted in unwarranted disparity excessively influenced by the personal views of the sentencing judge, and because I hoped that the proposed—now actual—guideline system would result in sentences which were effective and just. Today, I conclude, with sorrow and disappointment. . . . that the system is resulting in the imposition of many sentences which are neither just nor effective.

Judge Lasker criticized, among other things, the fact that sentencing guidelines do more than guide, they dictate. Judges are bound by a finite set of considerations when sentencing, and thus cannot exercise the discretion that the uniqueness of each case seems to require. Not included among these considerations are factors that many judges might find relevant in some cases, including the defendant's family ties and obligations. He pointed out, moreover, that sentencing guidelines give more power to prosecutors even as they take power away from judges. Since each offense has a corresponding sentencing range, the prosecutor—by choosing the charge on which to try the defendant, or engineering a plea agreement—can thus determine the sentencing range within which the judge may work.

But sentencing guidelines, Judge Lasker pointed out, do more than cause a power imbalance between judges and prosecutors. They also have resulted in a greater proportion of offenders going to prison, and in significantly longer prison sentences in general. This outcome may not be unquestionably undesirable, of course: one of the reasons that sentencing guidelines were originally created was the widespread belief that serious offenses were not drawing adequate punishments. Putting more people behind bars for longer periods of time, however, puts a serious strain on the criminal justice system that the system may not be able to bear for very long. The prison population in this country has been growing at an alarming rate since the 1980s, and the United States currently bears the dubious distinction of having a greater proportion of its people behind bars than any other nation. Prisons cost a huge amount of taxpayer money to run. We may like the idea of making violent, predatory criminals do hard time, but hard reality—in the form of limited space and limited resources—means that we have to be judicious in whom we imprison and for how long. Moreover, locking up criminals at the rate and for the lengthy terms that we do creates a negative

impression of American criminal justice from both outside and within. Some question whether "the land of the free" is still an apt name for a country that keeps more than 2 million of its people behind bars.

Another criticism of sentencing guidelines that Judge Lasker identified in his testimony is the fact that they operate through the manipulation of numbers, rather than the weighing and contemplation of a range of facts, values, and principles. Numbers have a certain appeal; they are less ambiguous, more consistent, and less "fuzzy" than preguideline judicial discretion. Judges who use numerical sentencing guideline values to produce sentences need only point to the calculations they performed to show that they used acceptable criteria in their decisions. But the problem with using such computations to arrive at sentences is that they make the sentencing process look more like a complex math problem than like justice being done. Consider the difference: without guidelines, the judge at a sentencing

The United States is known as "the land of the free." Critics wonder if the name is applicable when more than 2 million Americans are behind bars and the number is still growing.

hearing may explain the punishment meted out by citing as mitigating factors the defendant's youth, his lack of a prior record, and his family's reliance on his income; and as aggravating factors the brutality of the crime and the fact that the defendant lied to authorities about his role in it. With guidelines, the judge will cite the process of addition and subtraction that he or she used to calculate the precise length of the prison term that the defendant will have to serve. The latter version would appear more precise, perhaps.

The strict number-crunching process prescribed by the sentencing guidelines, even if it may seem overly mechanical, was designed to eliminate the disparities caused by judges' mistakes and abuse of discretion. But some studies have challenged the claim that sentencing guidelines even reduce disparity of sentences. Statistics collected by the Federal Sentencing Commission suggest that judges and probation officers apply the guidelines differently in different judicial districts, and that different plea-bargaining and charging practices in different areas often lead to different kinds of sentences in different jurisdictions. More than this, some critics have pointed out that the guidelines can be manipulated by shrewd defense attorneys and prosecutors. Having a sharp and hardworking lawyer can thus give a criminal defendant a decided advantage in the sentencing phase, because that lawyer may be able to argue for including a range of mitigating considerations that might otherwise be overlooked in the sentencing calculations. Poor defendants, however, are at a distinct disadvantage, because they are usually represented by overworked public defenders who may not have the time or experience necessary to angle aggressively for less severe sentences.

These findings point to the somewhat ironic results of sentencing guidelines. The movement against indeterminate sentencing emerged largely out of a concern that judicial discretion—whether because it led to sentencing disparities, or because it produced sentences that were not rigorous enough, or because it allowed for unreasonably lengthy incarcerations on the principle of rehabilitation—was undermining the public's faith in the courts and in American criminal justice. Now, however, we seem to have arrived at an impasse: the cure, by many accounts, is as bad as the disease. Is there a way out of this dilemma that Judge Lasker rightly characterizes as "disappointing"?

One judge, writing before the widespread adoption of sentencing guidelines, expressed the view that concern over judicial sentencing was missing the point. Trial judge Lois Forer, in her 1980 book *Criminals and Victims*, suggested that the concern with flaws in the sentencing process served to obscure larger problems in the priorities of the criminal justice system and of the government at large. She suggested that smarter laws and better allocation of resources would alleviate more problems within the system than sentencing reform could. Among her suggestions are stricter gun control laws, more resources devoted to education, and subsidized work programs for the chronically unemployed. These measures, argues Judge Forer, would prevent many of the episodes of property and violent crime that sentencing judges are forced to deal with after the fact.

Judge Forer, like many judges and other critics of recent sentencing reforms, also argues that sentencing laws that take judicial discretion away from judges altogether are more extreme than necessary in order to prevent abuses. Instead of restricting the activity of sentencing judges to the application of predefined numerical computations within narrow sentencing ranges, judges should be allowed to use the skill, knowledge, and wisdom that got them elected or appointed in the first place. The sentences they impose, however, should be subject to review by a higher court. Interestingly, as she points out, sentences—unlike nearly every other ruling by a trial judge—have historically not been open to appeal. Judge Forer writes, "Appellate review is the time-honored

Is the sentencing guideline "cure" as bad as the "disease"? These prisoners are stacked three beds high in a prison gymnasium because of a lack of cell space.

procedure by which common-law courts correct errors and abuses of discretion and develop the law. The opinions of higher courts provide the rationale for decision making which guides the trial bench and the bar. It is likely that if sentencing had been reviewable during the last century, a substantial body of law would have been created by federal and state appellate courts establishing criteria for sentencing. Legal scholars and criminologists would not today be frantically proposing drastic remedies which cut against the grain of the law."

Judge Lasker seconds Judge Forer's motion. Arguing that sentencing guidelines should be scaled back so that they are, in fact, merely guidelines rather than hard-and-fast rules, he then suggests that when and if judges choose to diverge from the guidelines, they should both have to justify their divergence and expect that their sentences will be appealed on the grounds that they abused their discretion.

Putting judges on notice that their sentences will be subject to legal challenge if they appear to deviate from generally recognized limits of justice and fairness might be a way of preventing the worst abuses and mistakes produced in the sentencing process. If such a system were put into effect, however, it might first be necessary to investigate exactly what proportion of sentences would in this case be subject to appellate review—and just how many defendants would in fact pursue an appeal. It may turn out that allowing review of sentences would put a huge burden upon the appellate court system. How far are we willing or obligated to go to allow defendants to challenge their sentences, especially if it were to result in a significant backlog of cases in the appeals courts?

Another question such a scheme would raise is whether, and by what criteria, appellate courts would be able to evaluate whether the sentencing judge had abused or justly employed his or her discretion in diverging from guidelines. Would the higher court have access to the same information that the trial judge had used? Would it consult records of prior sentences to see whether such divergences had ever been employed in the past?

In the end, the possibility of appellate review of sentencing decisions might have a chilling effect on the use of judicial discretion. Rather than taking the chance of having their decisions challenged, judges might be likely to adhere closely to the guidelines even if they thought that some divergence was justified. It's thus altogether possible that very little actual difference in sentencing outcomes would result from relaxing the guidelines and allowing appellate review of sentences.

Such a plan, however, even if it has relatively little material impact, might be an acceptable compromise between the systems of unfettered judicial discretion and rigid mathematical controls on the sentencing decisions. Judges would probably be satisfied knowing that they had more say in the sentences they imposed. They would also likely be glad that the controls placed on their sentencing choices would come from their colleagues on the higher courts, and would therefore be based on the principles of justice and fairness that guide their own judicial decision-making. Those who had originally objected to the lack of limits on sentencing, for their part, would welcome the imposition of accountability on the actions of the trial judge.

Whether such a proposal would be an acceptable compromise is one question; whether it would solve the flaws in the sentencing process is another. But this question, while perhaps an important one, may not be the most useful question to ask. Taking everything you now know about the sentencing process, can you imagine a truly flawless system of sentencing? What would such a system look like?

The history of our legal system has shown us that while we may, and must, strive to make laws that are completely just and fair, we can't always foresee the problems that may arise in trying to apply them in certain situations. Likewise, the people charged with interpreting and enforcing the laws may face dilemmas for which any of the available solutions would be in some way unsatisfactory. Judges are far from infallible; despite their experience, training, and wisdom, they can make mistakes and fail to see the most just and fair choice. But to take away discretion from judges by creating a system of numerically based rules is not a way out of the problem: those numbers, after all, are themselves the product of the imperfect humans on the sentencing commissions. It seems as if no solution exists that would allow us to avoid the problems that come from our innate shortcomings.

Is this really the insoluble dilemma that it seems to be? Instead of regretting the flaws in our system, or even resigning ourselves to them, perhaps we should use them to point us in a more positive direction. Having discovered that neither total judicial discretion nor the technical application of numerical calculations gives us a sentencing scheme we can embrace, we're forced to

seek out other methods. The quest for the best means of making the punishment fit the crime is not likely to be easy, nor is it ever really likely to come to an end. Social and political changes may continue to force us to rethink how, and even why, we impose the punishments we impose on criminals. If, for instance, we now think explicitly about punishment as intended both to deter future crimes and to inspire respect for the law, we might try to design a system that maximizes the certainty of punishment for violating the rules, but that ensures that the sentences we impose express respect for the rights of all citizens—even those who break the law. The process by which we try to get as close as we can to a completely fair system of punishment might not only be a way of ensuring that justice is done; it might also be one important way of doing justice.

A completely fair system of punishment may be unattainable, but continually moving toward that goal may be the best way to ensure that justice is done.

Bibliography

"Boesky Gets 3-Year Prison Term for Insider Trading." *Los Angeles Times*, December 20, 1987.

Chapin, Bradley. *Criminal Justice in America, 1606–1660*. Athens, Ga.: University of Georgia Press, 1983.

Copeland, Libby. "Kemba Smith's Hard Time." *Washington Post*, February 13, 2000.

Della Rocca, Fernando. *Manual of Canon Law*. Milwaukee: Bruce Publishing Co., 1959.

Forer, Lois G. *Criminals and Victims: A Trial Judge Reflects on Crime and Punishment*. New York: W. W. Norton, 1980.

French, Ron, and Doug Durfee. "Japanese Woman Sent to Psychiatric Hospital; Judge Calls Sentence in Baby's Drowning Most Agonizing She's Imposed." *The Detroit News*, October 11, 1996.

Friedman, Lawrence M. *Crime and Punishment in American History*. New York: Basic Books, 1993.

Gross, Hyman, and Andrew von Hirsch, eds. *Sentencing*. New York: Oxford University Press, 1981.

Jackson, Bernard S. *Essays in Jewish and Comparative Legal History*. Leiden, Netherlands: E. J. Brill, 1975.

Kaufman, Irving R. "Sentencing: The Judge's Problem." *Atlantic*, January 1960.

Klein, Andrew R. *Alternative Sentencing: A Practitioner's Guide*. Cincinnati: Anderson Publishing Co., 1988.

Krikorian, Greg, "Judge Slashes Life Sentence in Pizza Theft Case." *Los Angeles Times*, January 29, 1997.

Meyer, Jon'a, and Paul Jesilow. *"Doing Justice" in the People's Court: Sentencing by Municipal Court Judges*. Albany, N.Y.: SUNY Press, 1997.

Miller, Marc L., and Ronald F. Wright. "Your Cheatin' Heart(land): The Long Search for Administrative Sentencing Justice." *Buffalo Criminal Law Review* 723 (1999).

Bibliography

Mitford, Jessica. *Kind and Usual Punishment: The Prison Business.* New York: Vintage, 1974.

Remarks of Morris E. Lasker before the Symposium on Sentencing Guidelines, September 9, 1997. *http://www.sentencing.org/lasker.html.*

Saunders, Debra J. "Cruel and Unusual." *San Francisco Chronicle,* December 14, 1997.

Schwartz, Robert. "Make Way for Landlord; For Tenants, It's Not a Sentence, It's Home." *Los Angeles Times,* June 19, 1985.

Stith, Kate, and José A. Cabranes. *Fear of Judging: Sentencing Guidelines in the Federal Courts.* Chicago: University of Chicago Press, 1998.

"Tax Crime, Prison Time." *New York Times,* April 15, 1992.

Ulmer, Jeffery T. *Social Worlds of Sentencing: Court Communities Under Sentencing Guidelines.* Albany, N.Y.: State University of New York, 1997.

United States Sentencing Commission, *Guidelines Manual,* §3E1.1 (November, 1998).

Vick, Karl, and John Craddock. "Does Harsh Sentence Fit Milken's Crime?" *St. Petersburg Times,* November 22, 1990.

Wheeler, Stanton, Kenneth Mann, and Austin Sarat. *Sitting in Judgment: The Sentencing of White-Collar Criminals.* New Haven: Yale University Press, 1988.

Wicharaya, Tamasak. *Simple Theory, Hard Reality: The Impact of Sentencing Reforms on Courts, Prisons, and Crime.* Albany, N.Y.: SUNY Press, 1995.

Wright, Ronald F. "The Future of Responsive Sentencing in North Carolina." 2 *Federal Sentencing Reporter* 215.

Index

Index

Picture Credits

SARA MANAUGH is a scholar in the fields of law, philosophy, public policy, and popular culture. She holds a doctorate in Rhetoric from the University of California at Berkeley and is currently studying law at Columbia University.

AUSTIN SARAT is William Nelson Cromwell Professor of Jurisprudence and Political Science at Amherst College, where he also chairs the Department of Law, Jurisprudence and Social Thought. Professor Sarat is the author or editor of 23 books and numerous scholarly articles. Among his books are *Law's Violence*, *Sitting in Judgment: Sentencing the White Collar Criminal*, and *Justice and Injustice in Law and Legal Theory*. He has received many academic awards and held several prestigious fellowships. He is President of the Law & Society Association and Chair of the Working Group on Law, Culture and the Humanities. In addition, he is a nationally recognized teacher and educator whose teaching has been featured in the *New York Times*, on the *Today* show, and on National Public Radio's *Fresh Air*.